DIGITAL
TECHNOLOGIES
AND LEARNING
IN THE EARLY YEARS

Sara Miller McCune founded SAGE Publishing in 1965 to support the dissemination of usable knowledge and educate a global community. SAGE publishes more than 1000 journals and over 800 new books each year, spanning a wide range of subject areas. Our growing selection of library products includes archives, data, case studies and video. SAGE remains majority owned by our founder and after her lifetime will become owned by a charitable trust that secures the company's continued independence.

Los Angeles | London | New Delhi | Singapore | Washington DC | Melbourne

DIGITAL TECHNOLOGIES AND LEARNING IN THE EARLY YEARS

Edited by

LORNA ARNOTT

Los Angeles I London I New Delhi
Singapore I Washington DC I Melbourne

Los Angeles | London | New Delhi
Singapore | Washington DC | Melbourne

SAGE Publications Ltd
1 Oliver's Yard
55 City Road
London EC1Y 1SP

SAGE Publications Inc.
2455 Teller Road
Thousand Oaks, California 91320

SAGE Publications India Pvt Ltd
B 1/I 1 Mohan Cooperative Industrial Area
Mathura Road
New Delhi 110 044

SAGE Publications Asia-Pacific Pte Ltd
3 Church Street
#10-04 Samsung Hub
Singapore 049483

Editorial Arrangement © Lorna Arnott 2017
Chapter 1 © Lorna Arnott 2017
Chapter 2 © Eleni Karagiannidou 2017
Chapter 3 © Nicola Yelland and Caja Gilbert 2017
Chapter 4 © Lorna Arnott, Pauline Duncan and Deirdre Grogan 2017
Chapter 5 © Kelly Johnston and Kate Highfield 2017
Chapter 6 © Rachael Levy and Nathalie Sinclair 2017
Chapter 7 © Jane O'Connor 2017
Chapter 8 © Jo Bird 2017
Chapter 9 © Marilyn Fleer 2017
Chapter 10 © Susan Danby 2017

Editor: Jude Bowen
Editorial assistant: George Knowles
Production editor: Victoria Nicholas
Copyeditor: Jane Fricker
Marketing manager: Dilhara Attygalle
Cover design: Wendy Scott
Typeset by: C&M Digitals (P) Ltd, Chennai, India
Printed in the UK

Library of Congress Control Number: 2016953861

British Library Cataloguing in Publication data

A catalogue record for this book is available from the British Library

ISBN 978-1-41296-242-1
ISBN 978-1-41296-243-8 (pbk)

For Heather Arnott and Rebecca Arnott.
My daughters, my inspiration.

CONTENTS

EDITOR AND CONTRIBUTOR BIOGRAPHIES

The Editor

Lorna Arnott is a Lecturer in the School of Education, University of Strathclyde. Lorna's main area of interest is in children's early experiences with technologies, particularly in relation to social and creative play. She also has a keen interest in research methodologies, with a specialist focus on consulting with children. At the University of Strathclyde, Lorna teaches on the BA (Hons) Childhood Practice, The Early Years Pedagogue as part of the modular Master's of Education, BA (Hons) Education and the PGDE course. Lorna is the convener for the Digital Childhoods Special Interest Group as part of the European Early Childhood Educational Research Association and is the Editorial Assistant for the *International Journal of Early Years Education.*

The Contributors

Jo Bird is Lecturer in the School of Education at the University of New England, Armidale, Australia. She is about to submit her PhD at Australian Catholic University in Melbourne, Australia on children's use of technologies in their imaginative play and educators' influence on their provision of these devices. Jo was an educator in early childhood settings for over 15 years prior to becoming a teacher educator. Her research interests include children's play, learning and the use of technologies in early childhood education. She is currently serving as the Associate Editor (Early Years) for the *Digital Learning and Teaching Victoria Journal.*

Susan Danby is Professor in the School of Early Childhood at Queensland University of Technology (QUT), Australia. Her research investigates children and young people's everyday social and interactional practices, across a range of contexts, including preschool and school, family, helplines and clinical settings. Her recent research investigates how young children integrate digital technologies into the flow of everyday family and school lives. She has a co-edited book on children's disputes (2012), and she is on the editorial boards of *Children and Society, Linguistics and Education, Journal of Early Childhood Literacy* and *Research on Children and Social Interaction.*

Pauline Duncan is a Postdoctoral Researcher in the Moray House School of Education, University of Edinburgh. She is currently teaching on the departmental course on Developmental Psychology and working on two projects relating to young children and technology: 'Children and the Internet of Things' and 'Digital Technologies for Infants (0–3): Understanding Interaction with iPads in the Home'.

Marilyn Fleer is Professor and holds the Foundation Chair of Early Childhood Education and Development at Monash University, Australia, and the immediate past President of the International Society for Cultural Activity Research (ISCAR). Her research interests focus on early years learning and development, with special attention on pedagogy, culture, science and technology. More recently she has investigated child development in the contexts of home and school. Key publications are: *Early Learning and Development: Cultural-Historical Concepts in Play* (Cambridge University Press, 2010), *Play, Leaning and Children's Development: Everyday Life in Families and Transition to School* (with Mariane Hedegaard; Cambridge University Press, 2013) and *Theorising Play in the Early Years* (Cambridge University Press, 2014). Professor Fleer has been shortlisted for the Australian awards for Excellence in Educational Publishing and has received a commendation for outstanding postgraduate supervision from the Vice Chancellor of Monash University.

Caja Gilbert is a Research Officer at Victoria University, Melbourne, Australia, and a PhD Candidate at The University of Melbourne. Her research focuses on the impact of new technologies on the news media industry. More specifically, on how they affect journalistic practice and news content in our contemporary society.

Deirdre Grogan is Senior Lecturer in the School of Education, University of Strathclyde, with research interests in creativity and early years education. She is responsible for the Early Years module (Bachelor of Education), where students participate in a nursery placement, and is also involved in early years knowledge exchange courses with various local authorities.

Kate Highfield is a Research Fellow at the Research Institute for Professional Practice, Learning and Education at Charles Sturt University, Australia. Kate has extensive experience working with student teachers, children and educators in the fields of technology, as well as over 10 years' experience teaching in classrooms. Her PhD research focused on the use of simple robotics in mathematics learning and examined the key role of metacognition in problem solving. Her current research explores the use of interactive technologies for STEM learning and play, with a focus on how mobile and touch technology can be used as a tool to enhance learning. Kate is the editor of *Live Wires*, a publication for Early Childhood Australia.

Kelly Johnston is a Lecturer and PhD candidate at Macquarie University in Sydney, Australia. Kelly has extensive experience working in diverse early learning services and context across Australia, New Zealand and the UK. Her current teaching role is with student teachers at both undergraduate and postgraduate level on units relating to early childhood pedagogy, technology, theory and practice, and health and wellbeing. Her PhD research investigates educator conceptualisations of technology and practitioner enquiry as a professional learning model to support the integration of technology in early learning settings.

Eleni Karagiannidou is researching and teaching in the area of child development, problem-based learning, digital technologies, as well as teachers' and practitioners' professional learning and identity. Currently, as part of a funded project, she is examining professional identity, beliefs and practices of early years educators and associated impact on young learners. In the area of digital technologies, she is looking at participation in online communities, and the replication of identities, behaviours and cultures between offline and online environments.

Rachael Levy is a Lecturer in Early Childhood Education at the University of Sheffield. Her research interests include young children's perceptions of reading, home–school literacy discourses and multimodality. Rachael is also interested in the role of gender in literacy and the ways in which this connects with opportunity for all within the schooling system and beyond. She has a number of publications on these topics including her book *Young Children Reading at Home and at School* (Sage, 2011). She is currently leading a study within an ESRC collaborative project, to understand the barriers to shared reading in families.

Jane O'Connor is a Reader in Childhood Studies at Birmingham City University where she leads the 'Rethinking Childhood' research cluster. Jane began her career as a primary school teacher and moved into academia after completing a PhD on cultural constructions of child stars in the media. Her research interests focus on young children's use of media technology, 'exceptional' children and social constructions and representations of childhood. She has written and researched extensively on the topics of children and the media and child stardom and is currently leading an international study on the use of touchscreen technology by children under 3. Jane teaches on the doctoral programme at the university and supervises a range of PhD students.

Nathalie Sinclair is Professor in the Faculty of Education, an associate member in the Department of Mathematics and a Canada Research Chair in Tangible Mathematics Learning at Simon Fraser University. She is also an Associate Editor of *Digital Experiences in Mathematics Education*. She is the author of *Mathematics and Beauty: Aesthetic Approaches to Teaching Children* (Teachers College Press, 2006) and co-author of *Mathematics and the Body: Material Entanglements in the Classroom* (Cambridge University Press, 2014), among other books. Her research interests include the role of digital technology in the teaching and learning of mathematics, the changing ways in which the body is implicated in mathematical thinking and the aesthetic nature of mathematical enquiry.

Nicola Yelland is a Research Professor and Director of Research in the College of Education at Victoria University in Melbourne Australia. Over the last decade her teaching and research has been related to the use of new technologies in school and community contexts. Some recent publications are *Early Mathematical Explorations, Contemporary Perspectives on Early Childhood Education* (Oxford University Press, 2014) and *Rethinking Learning in Early Childhood Education* (Oxford University Press, 2009). She is also the author of *Shift to the Future: Rethinking Learning with New Technologies in Education* (Routledge, 2006). Professor Yelland is the founding editor of two journals *Contemporary Issues in Early Childhood* and *Global Studies of Childhood*.

ACKNOWLEDGEMENTS

As the contributors of the book have worked hard to ground their analysis and discussion in research evidence, this book could not have been completed without the help of the people who agreed to the research taking place in their settings. We would like to thank all educational settings, teachers, parents and children for their invaluable involvement.

I would also like to thank all the chapter authors for their contributions. Without them, this book would not have happened. I would especially like to express my appreciation for their patience in their work going to print to accommodate my period of maternity leave.

Many thanks must be extended to the great support offered by the Sage team: Jude Bowen and George Knowles. Similarly, their patience, flexibility, encouragement and support with the delay in this publication was overwhelming.

Finally, as always, the support of my family and in particular my husband, Campbell Arnott, has been unfaltering. I am eternally grateful for all that he does.

INTRODUCTION

Lorna Arnott

Children's engagement with technologies in everyday life, work and learning has altered perceptions of childhood. Product developers target the lucrative child market, and the abundance of child-friendly technological resources are now considered to be shaping contemporary childhood experiences in the West. Despite the lingering and iterative debates about technologies in childhood, advances in technological resources are progressing so quickly, and family experiences are so diverse, that we will never reach a consensus over the appropriateness of these resources for children. For this very reason, it is not the intention of this book to question the suitability of technologies for young children in their lives or in early years education and practice.

Digital Technologies and Learning in the Early Years will focus on showing how, from research evidence, children are using technologies as part of their life and learning and most specifically as part of their early play experiences and play-based pedagogies. It has been suggested that 'it is time for critical empirical and theoretical investigation of the contribution of digital devices in children's play and the opportunities offered for children to experiment with meanings' (Palaiologou, 2016: 307). In an attempt to begin this discussion, the authors draw on case study evidence to document the role of technologies in early childhood life, educational practice and play-based pedagogies. Given the breadth of focus within this book, the authors explore children's early experiences with technologies in formal and informal learning contexts. Similarly, the book discusses the use of a broad range of resources, both screen-based and non-screen-based. In doing so we address three central objectives which flow through each of the chapters:

1. To offer an evidence-based discussion of children's experiences with technologies in early years education and life, with direct links to early years pedagogy and play practices.
2. To broaden our understanding of technologies in early years education.
3. To detail the child's 'story' with technology.

The book is based upon the well-established approach to early years research and practice that seeks to locate the child at the centre. The focus is on detailing the child's experiences with technologies in the early years to drive practice forward. It is concerned with play-based pedagogical approaches and the position of technologies within this frame. Palaiologou (2016: 306) states that 'Play-based pedagogy is based on the ideology that play has motor, spatial, cognitive, emotional, social and moral values in children's development and is dependent on the idea of an active child who engages in actions that will lead to deep understanding and meaning making experiences.' The interactivity associated with technological resources suggests that play should be a central component of their use for all the reasons that Palaiologou suggests and examples of play experiences across the chapters in this book span the age ranges from 0–8 years. The work covers experiences in family homes, early childcare settings and early formal school provision.

Digital Technologies and Learning in the Early Years is presented in three parts:

Part 1 discusses 'The Early Years Technological Landscape'. This section focuses on digital childhoods in the broader sense. It focuses on the theoretical and societal issues around technology, including how we define technologies, what we mean by play with technologies and how technologies are shaping childhood. The three chapters in this section provide the theoretical base to help position the remaining discussion of children's play experiences in context. Across this part of the book, we seek to describe the contemporary landscape that is enriching children's early experiences, allowing them to learn beyond their physical environment.

In Chapter 1, 'Framing Technological Experiences in the Early Years', Arnott begins to unpick the fundamental question of what we mean by the term *technology* and what we mean by technological experiences, both at home and in early childhood practice. How we define technologies is fundamental to planning for technological experiences. In this book, we take a broad definition of technologies which moves beyond the personal computer, laptop and interactive whiteboard. By understanding technologies in a broader sense, we are able to see evidence of children's outdoor play with technologies, for example.

In Chapter 2, 'Children's Technological Learning Journeys', Karagiannidou grapples with the how technologies are shaping and transforming children's learning journeys, experiences and the concept of childhood in the broader sense. Contemporary children are faced with the prospect of negotiating and managing multiple identifies, for example, their embodied identity when face-to-face as well as their digital identity, forged for them initially by parents as part of social media and eventually managed by children as they transition towards using their own online spaces independently. This chapter offers some discussion about how this process is reshaping childhood as we know it.

Finally for this section, in Chapter 3, 'Re-imagining Play with New Technologies', Yelland and Gilbert describe how children's play experiences have become increasingly multimodal as a result of the integration of technologies into children's lives. These resources allow children to learn and play with concepts and ideas on multiple platforms in order to solidify understanding.

Part 2 deals with 'Children's Technological Experiences'. It is this part of the book where we seek to document the child's 'story' in relation to technological or digital play. These four chapters provide evidence of children using technologies as part of their play experiences with accompanying case studies. The focus is on detailing the ways in which technologies are used by children from current evidence to allow educators to inform their practice. The authors do not offer any judgements about whether technologies are beneficial or detrimental to children because the focus is on providing examples of technological experiences as well as how these may be framed and shaped by children and by adults. The authors work from the premise that technological affordances alone do not determine experiences.

In Chapter 4, 'Creative and Dramatic Play with Technologies', Arnott, Duncan and Grogan consider how children are able to utilise technological resources to express their creative thinking. The chapter begins by exploring how creative play with technologies may be defined before documenting a series of episodes of creative play with technologies from research evidence.

Chapter 5, 'Technology in Outdoor Play', offers innovative content by Johnston and Highfield as they tackle the notion of children using technologies outdoors. This is an area still in its infancy but it is a really lucrative avenue to explore, particularly in light of new applications and games which are being developed in a bid to tackle obesity and sedentary technology use. You only need to look to the recent Pokamon Go movement to see how children's digital play is moving outdoors.

In Chapter 6, 'Young Children Developing Literacy and Numeracy Skills with Technology', Levy and Sinclair tackle the age-old question of how technologies can contribute to cognitive development, in particularly literacy and numeracy. We see evidence of how children are able to interact with technologies to develop these concepts.

Finally, for this section of the book, in Chapter 7, 'Under 3s and Technology', O'Connor gives us a glimpse into the lives of very young children's technological play. There is growing interest in this underdeveloped area of research given the recognition that children under 3 are now readily engaging with internet-enabled devices.

Part 3, 'Supporting Playful Pedagogies with Technologies', returns to the macro-level discussions of young children's technology use. Unlike Part 1, which explored the lives of young children broadly, however, this final part of *Digital Technologies and Learning in the Early Years* offers a practice-based focus.

In Chapter 8, 'Children's Responses to Working and Non-Working Digital Technologies', Bird offers a novel discussion of technologies in practice by exploring non-working technologies (e.g. irons or hair straighteners which no longer function). This chapters extends our definition of technologies, opening up new possibilities for technological play and the use of 'technologies' in practice.

Chapter 9, 'Digital Pedagogy: How Teachers Support Digital Play in the Early Years', by Fleer extends the concepts discussed throughout the previous chapters in this book and solidifies thinking into a theoretical discussion of digital pedagogy. An invaluable read for those working with children in the contemporary digital era.

The final chapter in this book concludes by providing some insight into how all of these case studies, extracts of empirical data and theories are formed, by detailing children's technological journals in relation to research approaches. Chapter 10, 'Technologies, Child-Centred Practice and Listening to Children', by Danby addresses how technologies can be used to listen to children as well as the procedures that we need to follow in order to understand children's stories about technologies. It brings the book to a close by documenting some of the ways that children's technological stories are developed.

As much as possible, myself and the authors have attempted to present this book as an accessible bridge between theory, research evidence and practice in relation to children's technological play, while still maintaining a focus on the child's voice. Given the age range covered (0–8 years) and the infancy of some of the research foci, it has not always been possible to present the child's story from their own perspective, for example in O'Connor's chapter about under 3s play. Nevertheless, we hope that we have placed the child at the centre of all discussions by providing evidence of their play with technologies.

Reference

Palaiologou, I. (2016) Teachers' dispositions towards the role of digital devices in play-based pedagogy in early childhood education. *Early Years* 36(3): 305–321.

PART 1
THE EARLY YEARS
TECHNOLOGICAL
LANDSCAPE

1

FRAMING TECHNOLOGICAL EXPERIENCES IN THE EARLY YEARS

Lorna Arnott

CHAPTER OVERVIEW

Within the increasingly technologised landscape of early childhood experiences, this chapter sets the scene for the remainder of the book by considering how learning experiences are being shaped by the digital era. The chapter will articulate this discussion by following a young child through a snapshot in their learning journey with new technologies.

This chapter aims to:

- Set up the frame for understanding how play and learning experiences are moulded by the digital era.
- Set the scene for the remainder of the book by unpicking what in research and practice we could mean when discussing 'technologies'.
- Present a case study of a young child playing and learning with technologies.
- Consider the place for, and role of, 'technological experiences' in early childhood education.

Learning in the digital age

From childhood through to adulthood, life in Western society has become technologised (Plowman et al., 2010). The 'powerful informational, communicative and interactive learning possibilities' of technologies (Richards, 2006: 239) and the associated rapid changes in these technologies create a new landscape of knowledge, learning and growing up for young children. From the perspective of the child, the speed of technological developments and the pervasiveness of these resources in society and children's lives have led to a widespread polarised debate in both academic literature and the mass media. Some parents and academics continue to be concerned about the perceived dangers of too much technology for developing children (Palmer, 2015), while others have advocated the benefits of integrating technology into children's lives at young ages (Marsh et al., 2005; Saracho and Spodek, 2008). In adulthood, digital citizens and the digital workforce are embracing technologies in a bid for efficiency and higher productivity. As a result of the digital revolution and the increased expectation to be 'connected', the lines between personal and professional life are blurring. This is impacting on children as it is becoming increasingly common to hear arguments around children's digital literacy as a precursor for success in contemporary society. Certainly, academic literature suggests that in such a 'knowledge economy' and digital society children need to be well equipped to use technologies because they are likely to consume a large part of their working and personal life (Siraj-Blatchford and Siraj-Blatchford, 2006).

Thus, the presence of technologies in all aspects of our lives might be linked to changes in terms of how we construct and share knowledge, what counts as learning, as well as what counts as play. Questions have been raised about who owns knowledge in an open access, internet society, for example. Relatedly, in Chapter 2, Karagiannidou discusses how traditional learning theories are re-envisaged in light of the technological age, while, in Chapter 3, Yelland and Gilbert reflect on how play is being reimagined. The shift in perceptions across these chapters, and the remainder of the book, builds on long-standing research, theorising and discussions, which consider whether people learn differently in an age of bite-sized information and multitasking. For example, over a decade ago, it was suggested that 'Digital Natives' learn differently to those born prior to the 1980s (Prensky, 2001). This was developed and it is thought that increased use of technology from a young age legitimises learning through 'trial and error', 'tinkering' or 'bricolage' (Kolikant, 2010). The debate portrays contemporary children as multitasking, experiential learners, in contrast to previous generations who learned from slow, linear and step-by-step approaches (Prensky, 2001). This is not without challenge as some argue that it is not evidence-based (Bennett et al., 2008), but, nonetheless, the premise has laid roots as it calls for fundamental reform in teaching approaches. In light of this altered perception of children's learning experiences we are now seeing many of those from upper levels of schooling taking cues from long-standing early years principles. Thus, whether for better or for worse, technologies are shaping the trajectory of society and our educational experiences. It is fundamental for us to understand the role and place of these resources in everyday life and early years education.

Yet understanding the role and place of technologies in early years practice and in children's play experiences is fraught with challenge. First, definitions of technologies vary greatly among academics and practitioners, widening the theory–practice divide. While academics are beginning to adopt broad definitions of technologies encompassing more resources, such as early years programming resources (Bers and Horn, 2010), practitioners are still mainly focused on the use of tablet computers, cameras and interactive whiteboards. We need to understand better how we define technologies in both theory and practice before any mutual construction of principles and practices around technology for play in early childhood can be achieved.

Technology: Unpicking the term

In the Chapter Overview above, I write that this section discusses what we *could* mean when referring to technologies. I use this particular phrasing because a definition of technologies in relation to education and, in particular, early years education, is difficult to achieve. Elsewhere I have briefly explored the difficulties with defining technologies:

> In contemporary discussions of digital childhoods a range of nuanced terms are used to describe the resources children use as part of everyday life and learning including, but not limited to, 'technologies', 'digital technologies', 'Information and Communication Technologies (ICT)', 'smart toys', 'screen-based media' and 'digital media'. With such fast-paced evolution in technological resources, definitions quickly become erroneous. ... Research in relation to technologies has evolved through explorations of the desktop computer (Haugland, 1992), to 'electronically enhanced objects', 'clever' robotics (Bergen, 2008) and smart toys (Plowman, 2004) to screen-based media (Neumann and Neumann, 2014) and on to 'internet-enabled' resources (Palaiologou, 2016). ... These definitions are evolving and already calls for explorations of future technologies are in place, as Livingstone et al. (2015), suggests the need to explore 3D printing and Smart Homes. (Arnott, 2016b: 330)

Despite the brevity of the discussion in that particular chapter, in reality it warrants lengthier consideration due to its complexity. The interchangeable way that terminology is used to represent different resources, and the distinct difference in perspectives between researchers, academics and practitioners, make arriving at a universally accepted definition particularly difficult. This is especially troublesome when the aim of this book is to create a conduit between theory and practice, where it would be hoped that those generating theory and those applying said theory have come to a consensus.

One of the problems with defining technologies is the sheer volume and range of resources being covered. 'Digital media' and 'technology' are considered inclusive terms reflecting the range of resources likely to be available in early years education (Plowman, 2016). Such resources could include: music players and games consoles for entertainment purposes (McPake et al., 2013); everyday household technologies available to children, such as digital toys and games (Arnott, 2013; McPake et al., 2013); desktop and portable computers, including tablet computers and mobile devices (e.g. Edwards, 2013; Neumann and Neumann, 2014); 3D printers (Livingstone et al., 2015); non-screen-based resources such as microscopes and metal detectors (Savage, 2011); and now even non-working technologies, as Bird discusses in Chapter 8. Combining these examples, and the many more resources which are not listed above, into an encompassing list is almost impossible. For example, Plowman et al. (2010: 15) once suggested that technologies are 'electronic objects that are found in homes and educational settings'. Similarly, I have previously suggested that a usefully broad definition of technologies may be 'everyday electronic objects and toys that generate a response when stimulated by the child' (Arnott, 2013: 99). This definition served me well in relation to the technologies I was discussing for that particular project, but it does not offer a definition which could be universally applied to all technologies used in children's early playful experiences. Indeed, it is at odds with many of the technological devices discussed by the authors in this book, for example non-working technologies are not electronically powered and would not generate a response. According to the above definition, these recourses would be excluded but as we see from Bird's discussion, they offer valuable insight into how technologies are shaping children's play in contemporary early learning and childhood.

For that reason, much curricular or policy guidance has been known to offer an exemplar list of possible technologies to articulate their meaning (Scottish Executive, 2003) rather than present a comprehensive definition. This could be because the term 'technology' relates to innovation and with innovation not only come new resources but often a shift in focus. It is therefore not always achievable to have a static definition which fails to recognise these innovations. Instead an evolving list of sub-categories that could be used to describe the resources of interest to early years research and practice is often utilised. For example, there was once a strong focus on Information, Communication Technologies (ICT). As technologies involving new innovative resources have emerged, the use of ICT is slowly being replaced with the distinction between digital and non-digital. As computer scientists are taking a greater interest in education, we are seeing increased discussion of 'smart' resources and programmable artefacts which could be a category of technologies in their own right or could appear broadly under the 'digital' banner.

KEY DEFINITION

Digital devices

The term 'digital devices' is used here as a collective term for all equipment that contains a computer or microcontroller and to which adults and children might have access, a list which now includes toys, games consoles, digital cameras, media players and smartphones as well as handheld, laptop or desktop computers (Palaiologou, 2016b: 305).

Similarly, classification of resources as digital or technological *toys* in comparison to technological artefacts, devices, resources or tools (i.e. not a toy) is emerging.

Yet still the lines continue to blur as technologies evolve. In previous work, I have talked about non-toy technologies as *adult world resources* (e.g. digital cameras, metal detectors) (Savage, 2011), yet with the lucrative child technology market perpetually expanding, product developers are now producing children's versions of these adult world resources, such as toddler-friendly cameras or Digi Blue microscopes, designed specifically for children. These raise further questions over classification of resources once more. How do these varied categories of technologies shape children's play experiences and learning? In this book we would argue that narrow definitions of technology may limit the scope for technological play and misrepresent children's experiences.

In order to ensure breadth in children's technological play experience, we must ensure we adopt a broad-ranging perspective on technological resources. I have previously made the case that a clear definition is not as important as understanding the properties of the resources in question and recognising that children's experiences are always likely to be different.

> Irrespective of the definition employed, the central point to note is that technologies are heterogeneous (Bergen, 2008); they are not all the same. Indeed different resources offer different technological affordances (Carr, 2000) and as such may influence children's early experiences differently. In order to understand the role of technologies in early years, we must therefore consider the range of resources available and explore their affordances and unique properties. (Arnott, 2016b: 330)

I stand by this position but I also recognise that some guidance may be helpful to bridge the theory–practice divide. For that reason, I suggest that Johnston and Highfield's definition of technologies presented in Chapter 5 is particularly powerful.

KEY DEFINITION

Definition of technology

… anything that can create, store or process data – this could include digital toys or other devices such as computers or tablets (Palaiologou, 2016b); less tangible forms of technology such as the internet (Knight and Hunter, 2013); and imaginary technologies – such as those that appear in dramatic play (Edwards, 2014; Howard et al., 2012). (Johnston and Highfield, Chapter 5, p. 58)

Playing and learning with technologies

This book is concerned with how children's play experiences are evolving in light of the digital or technological era. In order to put the book in context it is useful to draw on an extended case study of a child's technological play experience in their early years. The story told here is my own, and my daughter's. I draw on my own experience living with two roles; as a mother concerned for my daughter's development, her future and her safety, and as an academic trying to maintain a balanced position on technologies in children's lives. I do not pretend that this case study is a result of rigorous research evidence (that comes from the remaining chapters in this book), but rather it is my reflection on a young girl's technological world. It represents some of the choices that we as parents need to make when raising our children in a constantly 'connected' world. It is also a world unregulated by learning outcomes – my focus for my daughter is for a happy and healthy childhood – so her experiences with technologies, presented in the case study below, are that of play and fun and self-motivation. As such the case study gives a useful introduction to the remaining chapters of this book because within this short snippet of informal childhood experience with technologies, we see every element of play experience, learning journey and, indeed, pedagogical considerations, which are so skilfully addressed by each chapter author.

CASE STUDY   A CHILD'S JOURNEY WITH TECHNOLOGIES FROM 0–3 YEARS

Heather will turn 3 years old in 3 months' time but already she is competent with digital touch screen internet-enabled technologies, and has been reasonably proficient for almost a year. When handed an unlocked mobile phone or iPad (or similar tablet), she can independently find Skype to call her grandmother or her father when he is away on business. She recognises the logo for Skype and when selected she can locate the appropriate contact from their contact image. She recognises the distinction between using Skype to video call and WhatsApp to send 'texts'. When she wants to 'text' she can locate the WhatsApp icon, locate the appropriate contact, typically her Grandmother, and she holds down the voice record function independently to send a 'text' (a voice message which is delivered instantly in the same way an SMS would be). She can make a standard voice call when the contacts have pictures (Figure 1). She can also locate the Spotify app on her own and select music. She can autonomously use YouTube. She can locate the app and select videos from the videos already available in the suggestion features (in the first instance she requires an adult to type in the search field for an appropriate video but when she returns to the app without the phone being completely shut down, the previous selection is still available). She can then seamlessly move to the next video from the list of suggestions offered by YouTube. Sometimes she watches videos intently and other times she 'browses', i.e. watches a video for a few minutes before moving on to the next. She can recognise the various icons for different apps and can remember where different TV programmes can be found. For example, on the iPad she can locate Ben and Holly in the videos icon because it was purchased from iTunes. When she wants to watch *Despicable Me*, she recognises that this is found in the Amazon Video icon and navigates to it (Figure 2).

Figure 1.1   Phoning Nanna to say thank you for the new pram

Figure 1.2   Long train journey with the iPad

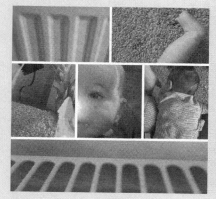

Figure 1.3   Photographs taken by Heather at 2 years old

Figure 1.4   Printing out a photograph with Polaroid Instant Print Camera

Figure 1.5   Hoovering the car with Dad

Figure 1.6   Shopping with her younger sister

(Continued)

(Continued)

Heather's use of these resources is balanced with other play activities. Throughout the day she also uses puzzles and paints or uses art materials to create pictures. She also uses digital 'paint' applications. She takes photographs and shows these to family and friends with pride, just as she does with her drawings and paintings (Figures 3 and 4). She plants vegetables in the garden with her father. She attends swimming lessons. She has a doll which she cares for in the same way I care for her little sister. She watches toy reviews, often of dolls and how they can be played with, fed and bathed like real babies, and has developed American terminology, such as diaper instead of nappy for American toys. She has a North American doll which is the same as one she watches on YouTube and she asks for a diaper for her but a nappy for her sister or all other dolls in the house. She attends nursery. She reads books at bedtime. She enjoys water play in the garden and she enjoys carrying out simple household jobs like washing the car or hoovering; she has a toy Dyson hoover, that actually vacuums – the same as her parents' (Figure 5). She bakes in her kitchen with her battery powered free-standing mixer, just as she bakes with me. She watches cooking programmes, such as how to bake Peppa Pig cakes, and she looks at paper recipe books. She plays with multi-coloured building blocks or shape sorters and watches videos of foods or toys separated into colours. She rides a balance bike. She visits the zoo or local farms and she takes pictures when she's out on excursions. She attends local museums. She pretends to buy and sell items using her shopping till and she has her mother's old cancelled credit card to 'purchase' goods (Figure 6). She likes to scan the barcode of items on self-service machines when out shopping with her family. She goes to the park and spends hours climbing, swinging and sliding. She has a family dinner time where she talks about her day. She has an old landline telephone handset that no longer works and she role-plays conversations with it. She walks to see the horses in the fields. She attends BookBugs sessions at her local library.

The examples presented above give only a snapshot of Heather's experiences but even so, it is clear that technologies are plentiful in Heather's world, yet not overpowering. Heather's motivation to engage with technologies is self-initiated. Despite my research focus in my academic role – which some might assume would lead me to encourage more technology use – I have to ensure balance in Heather's activities to avoid overuse of sedentary technology engagement, just as any other parent. It is for that reason, and from my previous research knowledge (Arnott, 2013; Arnott, 2016a; Arnott, 2016b; Arnott et al., 2016), that I called this chapter framing technological experiences in early years. High quality experiences with technologies do not happen by chance. Technologies do not do the pedagogic planning for us, despite their interactive properties. Yet we see from the short case study above how, through open ended play and fun, carefully framed, scaffolded and supported experiences, children can have enriched technological journeys.

The role of technological experience in early childhood education

What is clear from this case study, and potentially of most relevance to this book, is that children incorporate technologies into their play experiences naturally, based on what they see in the lives around them – the way children have always done with traditional resources. Just as Heather breastfeeds her doll after seeing her sister being fed, Heather uses technologies in the way her parents do, i.e. she walks around the house talking on her pretend phone while simultaneously cooking, or pushing the pram. She copies her parents' actions when she takes a photo of her sister by clicking her fingers above her head to get her attention. She scans her library books with the LED light of a desktop mouse just the way librarian does when taking books out of the library. For Heather, technologies are all around her. She integrates them into her play in the same way she would with traditional resources.

What does all this mean for technological experiences in early years education, learning and play? Elsewhere I have described how technologies could be integrated skilfully into early childhood practice and life.

> Gripton argues that part of supporting child-initiated play and learning is planning for endless possibilities. She argues that 'preparing and enabling endless possibilities is as much about belief and faith as it is about the practicalities' (2013: 18). The same is true for technologies, which should be viewed as another resource in your setting through which you can plan for 'opportunities' (Savage, 2011), 'possibility thinking' (Craft, 2012) and 'endless possibilities' (Gripton, 2013). Balance the risks, but embrace the potential afforded by technologies and utilise them in a manner that suits your practice and children's learning – just as you already do with traditional resources! (Arnott, 2016b: 338)

With digital technologies permeating early years playrooms and homes, there is a perception that these resources alter early years practice in some way. That parents and practitioners need to be vigilant with technological toys. The focus on technologically-specific practice is fuelled by the interpretation that technologies are unique resources, which bring with them their own specialist set of requirements in children's learning. Technologies are consistently segregated in policy and curriculum documents as distinct, stimulating the discussion about how these resources should be integrated into children's lives. Yet how different are these artefacts? And what different impact do they really have on children's early experiences in comparison to traditional early years toys and resources?

One argument for the lack of exploration of technologies in context may be that, in fact, these children used technologies differently in preschool to other traditional playroom resources. Certainly, evidence suggests that technologies, computers in particular, were not well integrated into play-based curricula (Howard et al., 2012). While calls for more developmentally appropriate use of technologies in early childhood playrooms are evident (Parette et al., 2010), until recently the lack of understanding around technology as part of play-based curricula makes this challenging. Howard et al. (2012) demonstrate the inherent issues of integrating technologies into the playroom by highlighting that research recommends that technology use should be guided by adults. In doing so, they argue, you are formalising the activity and reducing the play-based, child-initiated nature of the activity. In recent years, however, this perception is changing and was are seeing more play-based experiences with technologies.

This short story of Heather's experience gives us insight into how the experiences considered in this book may unfold in a child's life.

1. We begin to understand Heather's technological learning journey is one of participation and co-construction as she constructs digital conversations or takes photographs (Chapter 2).
2. We see multimodal play as Heather watches baking videos, plays with toy baking equipment and bakes real cakes with me (Chapter 3).
3. We see creativity and dramatic play as Heather engages in digital and traditional art activities or acts out role-play scenes (Chapter 4).
4. We see technologies used outdoors as she acts as a photographer in museums or when on excursions (Chapter 5).
5. Numeracy and literacy are highly developed through watching colour matching videos or toy reviews. Many vloggers record themselves separating out confectionary, such as bags of M&Ms into the groups of colours. They edit these videos to music and insert text which shows how the colour of that particular group of M&Ms looks when it's written. In other cases, children watch videos of people opening toy packaging or surprise eggs and these eggs are often colour coded to help children learn the colours as they watch. Literacy is also developed in this manner and it was interesting to see that Heather uses terminology appropriately in different contexts (Chapter 6).
6. Given Heathers proficiency with YouTube, she was often able to navigate to materials that were not appropriate. These were still child orientated videos but they may represent behaviours by other children on the videos which we as parents considered to be offensive. Alternatively, she might navigate to nursery rhymes that she was not allowed watch, such as Three Little Pigs, because the wolf had proven to give her nightmares. This gave us the opportunity to begin to instil an understanding of safe internet use. Heather discussed the inappropriate videos and her recognition of safety became apparent when she began saying at the beginning of an iPad session: 'I won't watch the nasty ones, promise'. Her viewing is still monitored but access to the device was not rescinded because of inappropriate content. The regulation of children's use of online social spaces by relevant legislation, parental control and product development limits their opportunities for 'testing boundaries, socializing and for taking risks in safe way' (Bers, 2012: 3). Guided internet use by us provides this opportunity. All of these experiences represent the world of a child under 3 years old and the associated decision making of the adults responsible for her care (Chapter 7).

7. She demonstrates interchangeable use of working and non-working technologies, understanding clearly when her non-working telephone handset requires pretend play rather than interactive two-way conversation over a working telephone. She uses an old discarded credit card for pretend play but doesn't ask to use it in shops. (Chapter 8).

8. The framing of these activities by me demonstrate a form of digital pedagogy when adopting a broad definition of pedagogue, a process which is fundamental to children's technological play and underpins every aspect of the learning experience (Chapter 9).

9. The self-motivated nature of Heather's play reflects how we can incorporate technological leaning experiences in a child-centred way by listening to their interests and needs. Permission was granted by Heather to Print her pictures and tell her story. (Chapter 10).

SUMMARY

To integrate technologies into play-based approaches skilfully it is important to consider the affordances of new technologies, alongside the possibilities and challenges they pose. Their interactive, immersive nature, use of powerful multimedia, user-generated and communication-enabling characteristics allow children to interact with new multifaceted learning environments and with other learners in a global community. This aids their cognitive, social and emotional development, and increases their self-efficacy and academic achievement (e.g. Sung and Hwang, 2013). Nowadays, possibly more than ever, children of all ages are not merely consumers of knowledge but rather contributors and co-constructors of collective experiences and meaning (Fischer and Konomi, 2007). Yet it seems that educators still do not believe this to be true:

> Teachers considered their use to be in opposition to what they actually try to do, believing that digital devices do not create opportunities for play in which children explore all their senses, but tend to limit both language interaction and opportunities for self-directed actions. (Palaiologou, 2016b: 316)

In reality the nature of play is changing in the digital era (Marsh et al., 2016). This book begins to give some insight to contemporary technological and digital play and fundamentally the digital pedagogy associated with these experiences.

References and further reading

Arnott, L. (2013) Are we allowed to blink? Young children's leadership and ownership while mediating interactions around technologies. *International Journal of Early Years Education* 21(1): 97–115.

Arnott, L. (2016a) An ecological exploration of young children's digital play: Framing children's social experiences with technologies in early childhood. *Early Years* 36(1): 271–288.

Arnott, L. (2016b) The role of digital technologies. In: I. Palaiologou (ed.), *Early Years Foundation Stage: Theory and Practice* 3rd ed. London: Sage, pp.329–342.

Arnott, L., Grogan, D. and Duncan, P. (2016) Lessons from using iPads to understand young children's creativity. *Contemporary Issues in Early Childhood* 17 (2): 1–17.

Bennett, S., Maton, K. and Kervin, L. (2008) The 'digital natives' debate: A Critical review of the evidence. *British Journal of Educational Technology* 39(5): 775–786.

Bergen, D. (2008) New technologies in early childhood: partners in play? In: O.N. Saracho and B. Spodek (eds), *Contemporary Perspectives on Science and Technology in Early Childhood Education*. Charlotte, NJ: Information Age Publishing, pp.87–104.

Bers, M.U. (2012) *Designing Digital Experiences for Positive Youth Development: From Playpen to Playground*. New York: Oxford University Press.

Bers, M.U. and Horn, M.S. (2010) Tangible programming in early childhood. In: I.R. Berson, and M.J. Berson (eds), *High-tech Tots: Childhood in a Digital World*. Charlotte, NJ: Information Age Publishing, pp. 49–70.

Carr, M. (2000) Technological Affordance, social practice and learning narratives in an early childhood setting. *International Journal of Technology and Design Education* 10(1): 61–80.

Craft, A. (2012) Childhood in a digital age: Creative challenges for educational futures. *London Review of Education* 10(2): 173–190.

Edwards, S. (2013) Digital play in the early years: A contextual response to the problem of integrating technologies and play-based pedagogies in the early childhood curriculum. *European Early Childhood Education Research Journal* 21(1): 199–212.

Edwards, S. (2014) Towards contemporary play: Sociocultural theory and the digital-consumerist context. *Journal of Early Childhood Research* 12(3): 219–233.

Fischer, G. and Konomi, S.I., (2007) Innovative socio-technical environments in support of distributed intelligence and lifelong learning. *Journal of Computer Assisted Learning*, 23(4): 338–350.

Gripton, C. (2013) Planning for endless possibilities. In A. Woods (ed.), *Child-Initiated Play and Learning: Planning for Possibilities in the Early Years*. London: Taylor & Francis.

Haugland, S.W. (1992) The effect of computer software on preschool children's developmental gains. *Journal of Computing in Childhood Education* 3(1): 15–30.

Howard, J,, Milesm G,E, and Rees-Davies, L. (2012) Computer use within a play-based early years curriculum. *International Journal of Early Years Education* 20(2): 175–189.

Knight, K. and Hunter, C. (2013) *Using Technology in Service Delivery to Families, Children and Young People*. CFCA Paper No. 17. Australian Institute of Family Studies, Child Family Community Australia. Retrieved from: http://aifs.gov.au/cfca/pubs/papers/a145634/ (accessed 27 January 2017).

Kolikant, Y. (2010) Digital natives, better learners? Students' beliefs about how the Internet influenced their ability to learn. *Computers in Human Behavior* 26(6): 1384–1391.

Livingstone, S., Marsh, J., Plowman, L., et al. (2015) *Young Children (0–8) and Digital Technology: UK Report*. Luxenbourg: Publications Office of the European Union.

Marsh, J., Brooks, G., Hughes, J., et al. (2005) *Digital Beginnings: Young Children's Use of Popular Culture, Media and New Technologies*. Sheffield: University of Sheffield.

Marsh, J., Plowman, L., Yamada-Rice, D., et al. (2016) Digital play: A new classification. *Early Years* 36(3): 242–253.

McPake, J., Plowman, L. and Stephen, C. (2013) Pre-school children creating and communicating with digital technologies in the home. *British Journal of Educational Technology* 44(3): 421–431.

Neumann, M.M. and Neumann, D.L. (2014) Touch screen tablets and emergent literacy. *Early Childhood Education Journal* 42(4): 231–239.

Palaiologou, I. (2016a) Children under five and digital technologies: Implications for early years pedagogy. *European Early Childhood Education Research Journal* 24(1): 5–24.

Palaiologou, I. (2016b) Teachers' dispositions towards the role of digital devices in play-based pedagogy in early childhood education. *Early Years* 36(3): 305–321.

Palmer, S. (2015) *Toxic Childhood: How The Modern World Is Damaging Our Children And What We Can Do About It*. London: Orion.

Parette, H. P., Quesenberry, A.C., and Blum, C. (2010) Missing the boat with technology usage in early childhood settings: A 21st century view of developmentally appropriate practice. *Early Childhood Education Journal*, 37(5): 335–343.

Plowman, L. (2004) 'Hey, hey, hey! It's time to play': Exploring and mapping children's interactions with 'smart' toys. In: J. Goldstein, D. Buckingham and G. Brougere (eds), *Toys, Games, and Media*. Mahwah, NJ: Lawrence Erlbaum.

Plowman, L. (2016) Learning technologies at home and preschool. In: N. Rushby and D. Surry (eds), *Wiley Handbook of Learning Technology*. Chichester: Wiley.

Plowman, L., Stephen, C. and McPake, J. (2010) *Growing Up With Technology: Young Children Learning in a Digital World*. London: Routledge.

Prensky, M. (2001) Digital natives, digital immigrants. *On the Horizon* 9(5): 1–6.

Richards, C. (2006) Towards an integrated framework for designing effective ICT-supported learning environments: the challenge to better link technology and pedagogy. *Technology, Pedagogy and Education* 15(2): 239–255.

Saracho, O.N. and Spodek, B. (2008) *Contemporary Perspectives on Science and Technology in Early Childhood Education*. Charlotte, NJ: IAP-Information Age Publishing.

Savage, L. (2011) *Exploring Young Children's Social Interactions in Technology-Rich Early Years Environments*. Institute of Education, Stirling: University of Stirling.

Scottish Executive (2003) *Early Learning, Forward Thinking: The Policy Framework for ICT in the Early Years*. Learning Teaching Scotland.

Siraj-Blatchford, I. and Siraj-Blatchford, J. (2006) *A Guide to Developing the ICT Curriculum for Early Childhood Education*. Stoke on Trent: Trentham Books Ltd.

Sung, H.-Y, and Hwang, G.-J. (2013) A collaborative game-based learning approach to improving students' learning performance in science courses. *Computers & Education* 63(4): 43–51.

2

CHILDREN'S TECHNOLOGICAL LEARNING JOURNEYS

Eleni Karagiannidou

CHAPTER OVERVIEW

The presence of technologies in childhood is so prolific in contemporary societies that entire working groups have been set up to research, debate and understand the role of technologies in children's lives. Some core questions explored include: Are there new opportunities for learning and teaching with digital technologies? Is learning itself being transformed because of the availability of technologies? Are new sets of skills required to be able to grow up, learn, live and work in a digital era? As a result of this work, terms like Digital Childhood, Digital Natives and TechnoTots are now relatively commonplace. It is argued that this activity suggests some form of shift in the conceptualisation of childhood and how children learn as a result of the presence of digital technologies in their young worlds. This chapter begins to explore these perceived changes to early childhood experiences and learning. It addresses four key themes:

- Access to technologies and internet-enabled resources in contemporary societies is increasing for young children, even in the early years; this is shaping but not determining their play and learning experiences.
- Children are believed to learn differently in light of the digital era, as technologies offer new ways of engaging with learning content in formal and informal learning contexts.
- Children of all ages are not merely consumers of knowledge, but rather contributors and co-constructors of collective experiences and meaning.
- Reaching an understanding of effective pedagogies that can support different forms and contexts of learning experienced by children in a digital era involves considering the meaning that children attribute to their learning and play experiences with new technologies.

Introduction

The proposition that children are growing up in a rapidly changing technological era that is distinctively different from that of their parents and grandparents is not a new one. Equally, the quest to understand how new technologies are transforming our learning experiences and lives is a long-standing one. Nevertheless, it remains invaluable, assisting us to understand and document the ways in which we can enhance children's potential for learning and development. While current trends in the literature focus mainly on older children, looking at the experiences and learning of younger children with new technologies has important methodological extensions and educational and policy implications. This chapter will follow young children of today through their learning journey with new technologies, and will discuss theoretical and practical frameworks for understanding their learning experiences.

New digital technologies?

From a historical point of view, the move from personal computers to the rather static World Wide Web and later to the Web 2.0 era is characterised by increasingly dynamic online interactions that put emphasis on user-generated content, and create platforms and opportunities for communication and dialogue between communities of users. The continuous, rather rapid developments in this field see us through a passage from Web 2.0 with its focus on the social nature of the Web, to the Web 3.0 era, which, as it is referred to by some, is a 'supposed third generation of Internet-based services', the so-called 'intelligent web' (Anderson and Whitelock, 2004; Morris, 2011).

KEY DEFINITION

Web 1.0, Web 2.0 and Web 3.0

Fuchs (2010: 764) refers to Web 1.0 as 'web of cognition', Web 2.0 as 'web of human communication' and Web 3.0 as 'web of cooperation'.

Turning to early years, specifically, and as discussed throughout this book, when thinking about 'new digital technologies' in a learning context, we could consider some of the associated technologies and tools and their affordances, including all kinds of technological toys, platforms, tools, resources and interactions. Even though the scope of this chapter is not to examine all these in detail, it is important to consider the affordances of new technologies, alongside the possibilities and challenges they pose.

Children as contributors and co-constructors of collective experiences and meaning

When considering 'new digital technologies' in a learning context we could refer to ways in which these have revolutionised the possibilities and processes of generating, collecting, consuming and disseminating information and knowledge, as well as interacting with the resources and each other on a global scale. Therefore the focus is not only on 'what' is generated or produced but also on 'how' it is generated, processed and experienced. This is not a new idea per se, as various theories of child development and learning highlight the role of experiences in learning. Yet nowadays, possibly more than ever before, children of all ages are not merely consumers of knowledge (Fischer and Konomi, 2007), but rather contributors and co-constructors of collective experiences and meaning. It is for this reason that new technologies, such as Web 2.0-like technologies, are viewed as creating a 'participatory culture' (Jenkins et al., 2009) and 'a new kind of participatory medium that is ideal for supporting multiple modes of learning' (Brown and Adler, 2008: 18). The concept of modality is expanded upon in the next chapter by Yelland and Gilbert. For this chapter, however, it is sufficient to say that these new networks of participation are also open to our youngest children, with children 3 years old or younger using internet-enabled resources, as demonstrated in the previous chapter's case study.

New pedagogies?

What is interesting about new digital technologies is their interactive potential, immersive nature, use of powerful multimedia and user-generated and communication-enabling characteristics. These allow children to experience and interact with new multifaceted learning environments and with other learners in global communities. With these affordances in mind, there is a line of enquiry exploring the links, latent or explicit, between digital technologies and learning. In this section, I will discuss some of the pedagogies that have been utilised to understand learning and teaching with new digital technologies. Drawing upon classic theoretical frameworks such as constructivism, social constructivism and social learning, situated learning and participatory learning models, as well as transformational play-based learning, I will discuss how new technologies in the early years cannot only inform pedagogical thinking in this period of life but also, from a child-focused perspective, enable children to engage with the 'art of learning' (Papert, 1991).

While developing this discourse, it is paramount to examine the role of modern 'pedagogues', parents, educators and other early years professionals, in supporting children through their learning journeys. The reasons for this are two-fold and interlinked. The first is focused on learners themselves. New technologies affect the physical, social, emotional, psychological, educational and learning 'environments' that surround children. In many cases, children are immersed in experiences with digital technologies before their formal schooling years, and they come to school equipped with an already developing range of skills and experiences (Craft, 2012). Therefore, one of the main reasons for this undertaking relates to the growing need for understanding the complexities of children's formal and informal learning experiences. The second reason relates to the role of early years pedagogues in exploring and supporting learning and teaching and in contributing to the creation of communities of pedagogical practice. Understanding what kinds of experiences with digital technologies bring about learning, how these are acted upon, and what associated learning theories can explain the processes involved, can inform a model of pedagogical practice that is evidence-based and theoretically meaningful. Most importantly, developmentally connected learning supported by digital technologies in the early years can transform not only practice, learning activities and experiences, but also relationships and roles among early years professionals, families, communities and children.

The main intention in this discourse is less to advocate my particular thesis and more to highlight the value of understanding the complexities of formal and informal learning experiences with new technologies and to contribute to a dialogue that focuses on improving the ways in which we can support children when building communities of learners. The discussion that follows does not claim that technology improves education by itself, nor does it aim to be comprehensive (e.g. relatively new epistemologies of e-learning, such as connectivism, are not discussed), but rather the intention is to contribute to the investigation of the ways in which 'digital technologies' can effectively inform and be informed by teaching and learning. In particular for this book, it aims to stimulate discussion and reflection on practice to enable us to better consider children's play experiences with technologies.

The behaviourist perspective

The theoretical underpinnings of this perspective lie in the work of early prominent behaviourists, such as Pavlov, Watson, Thorndike and Skinner. Focusing on observable and measurable behaviours rather than non-observable processes such as thinking, this perspective postulates that learning involves the process of forming associations between stimuli and responses, through mechanisms such as operant conditioning, and that learning and consequently knowledge, is, therefore, an organised accumulation of these associations.

Although this theory does not constitute one of the current prominent perspectives on learning, the underlying idea is evident in models of individualised instruction, which has 'underpinned the development of programmed instruction and computer programmes that teach routine skills' (e.g. an app teaching chess). This involves drills or routines of activities organised based on prior performance, where each learner 'responds actively to questions or problems and receives immediate feedback on their response' (Mayes and de Freitas, 2004: 8).

Constructivism and social learning frameworks

Even though the term 'constructivism' is used rather widely in educational literature and it provides the basis for several learning theories, the theoretical underpinnings of constructivism put emphasis on learner-centred learning, enquiry-based exploration and discovery, as well as continuous knowledge 'construction' via active learning and meaning-making. Quite often a distinction is provided between cognitive constructivism, traditionally linked to the Piagetian approach and ideas, and social constructivism, linked to the Vygotskian approach, which maintains that learning results from internalisation of ideas and practices encountered and experienced in the sociocultural realm (Duffy and Cunningham, 1996).

A relevant concept, is that of the zone of proximal development (ZPD) introduced by Lev Vygotsky. Emphasising the role of social interaction, it refers to the difference between what children can achieve alone and what they can achieve with assistance and support from others. Understanding contained within a child's zone of proximal development could emerge with the support of knowledgeable others. Linked to this is the concept of scaffolding, introduced by Wood et al. (1976); this highlights the importance of providing support in the initial stages of learning and removing it as learners become competent and confident. Also linked to this is the notion of collaborative learning and peer collaboration, which are seen as being constructivist in nature, since learning takes place as learners interact with each other and build on each other's ideas, concepts and knowledge; in other words, learners collaboratively construct experiences, understandings and meaning.

New digital technologies reflect social constructivist and social learning epistemologies in a variety of ways. In early years this quite often involves play-based learning experiences, and includes tools and practices that promote grounded interactions between communities of users around content, problems, or actions. Technology-infused or -enriched learning environments have the potential to encourage learners to become active participants in their own learning, engaging with self-regulation and reflecting on 'how' rather than 'what' they learn. In addition, they can provide learning opportunities that model peer-based collaborative knowledge construction, as well as collaborative tools and opportunities to promote not only cognitive scaffolding, but also affective or emotional scaffolding, by providing positive feedback which is either computer-based or user-generated and by sharing learning with others.

Situated learning

In line with the social constructivism perspective, the underpinnings of situated learning, which lie in the work of Lave and Wenger and their concept of 'legitimate, peripheral participation' (Lave and Wenger, 1991; Wenger, 1998), promote the idea that knowledge cannot be abstracted from the situations in which it is learned or used. It cannot be reached independently of context, but rather through active learning which needs to be situated in meaningful and authentic contexts and cultures.

As Brown et al. (1989: 34) note, from an early age, children are given the chance to 'observe and practise in situ the behaviors of members of a culture' and gradually adopt or learn these. Pointing to the ease with which these belief systems and behavioural norms are adopted, they highlight the importance of authentic contexts of learning, contrasting it to the explicit teaching that takes place within the frames of school-based 'inauthentic' activities and practices. Going beyond the walls of formal learning and the role of more explicit approaches to teaching, this perspective lends itself to approaches of teaching and learning that blend in-school and out-of-school learning, enabled by Web 2.0 technologies.

Participatory learning

Not dissimilar to some of the aforementioned perspectives, this framework sits within the sociocultural theoretical perspectives of learning supported by children's meaningful experience and participation in their families, communities and cultures. This perspective resides within John Dewey's school of thought, where learning is understood as a 'mode of activity on the part of the child which reproduces, or runs parallel to, some form of work carried in social life' (Dewey, 1915: 131).

Scholars within this framework emphasise learning as involving knowledge acquisition and participation, whereas others highlight the importance of creation in learning (Paavola et al., 2004). Hedges and Cullen (2012) argue that 'meaningful knowledge building occurs in the context of self-motivated participation in authentic activities' and that young children may 're-create and represent their knowledge in their collaborative play in early childhood settings'. This shapes their capacity to respond to the complexity of the world around them.

Associated with the Web 2.0 era, this framework views learning as a 'participatory, social process, supporting personal life goals and needs' that takes place in a 'digital world, with high connectivity and ubiquitous, demand-driven learning' (McLoughlin and Lee, 2007: 664). Because of the 'social software' affordances of current technologies, learning is embedded in a community of practice where the focus is 'both on "learning to be" through enculturation into a practice as well as on collateral learning' (Brown and Adler, 2008: 30). This 'demand-pull' informal learning, centres around the construction of knowledge and creation of 'artefacts' in collaborative, authentic and meaningful learning contexts. These contexts are underpinned by culturally grounded pedagogies. They support lifelong learning in both online and offline, as well as in- and out-of-school contexts.

Transformational play, experiential learning and game-based learning

A rather dominant path in current early childhood research and literature of navigating learning landscapes is via play. It is the focus of technological experiences in this book. As Hedges and Cullen (2012: 922) highlight, 'play is both a social and a cultural construct and a social practice that has defied straightforward definitions' and the literature around it is 'complex, ideological and contradictory'. Some have supported the idea that play creates a zone of proximal development for children and provides opportunities for meaningful and authentic learning, whereas others suggested that, as practised within curricula, integration of play often evolves around teacher-created and adult-led opportunities, with 'learning assumed to follow' (Hedges and Cullen, 2012: 922).

Play and its different forms make an interesting path to examining technology-infused learning. There are two aspects to this undertaking. One is concerned with building frameworks for understanding how children learn to use technologies through play, whereas the other relates to the questions that arise from adopting technology-infused play-based methods and approaches to promote learning. Some argue that these kinds of engagement fall within the realm of edutainment; in the case of game-based learning, as an example, it has been suggested that this form of learning does not readily support learners to make connections between knowledge learned in the game, and knowledge within and outside the school setting. Nevertheless, the opportunities offered by digital technologies for instigating curiosity, creativity, as well as opportunities for exploration of the physical, emotional and social worlds in which children operate and define should not be underestimated.

New technology-infused learning and teaching?

Digital technologies align rather well with several of the frameworks discussed above and associated curricula. Such frameworks invite the integration of individual and collaborative learning and encompass the role of educators, pedagogues and families in supporting children to engage with formal and informal learning communities. The technology-infused learning experiences and tools and their affordances discussed here have the potential to encourage engagement, active learning and creativity, and support social interaction.

As not all children learn in the same way, digital technologies can support learning experiences that are individualised and tailored to their diverse needs and varied interests. Many Web 2.0 applications provide the tools for such personalised experiences. For example:

- Allowing the learner to organise and share their thinking, there are various websites or applications that provide the tools for young learners to create content, for example, mind maps for any topic, which can then be shared with peers and adults. Numerous such websites or apps allow users to incorporate not only words, but also symbols, images, user-generated photographs and videos, thus not only making them suitable for younger learners but also supporting creativity. These can be exported to different file formats, and in some cases incorporated into other apps, allowing their re-use for a variety of purposes.
- Based on Web 2.0 technologies, online multi-user whiteboards provide a common space where text, files, drawings, photographs and videos can be shared between different users or groups of users, such as different classrooms. These encourage collaboration between young learners and can be used for subject-led projects or simply to brainstorm on group activities, and reach a shared understanding of the focus topic. Some tools also allow for user-initiated content evaluation by incorporating feedback systems. These tools' cross-platform and multi-purpose communication capabilities and affordances can capitalise on the learning that peer interaction entails and can facilitate diverse forms of scaffolding.
- Similarly, collaborative multimedia slide-show tools are suited to young learners. Commonly these can incorporate user-generated multimedia. They can be used for individual and group school or home projects. Some tools provide the option to record narration or comments. Using such tools with inexperienced or

shy learners can provide opportunities for individualised or small-group feed-back and support them as they work not only on their understanding of the subject matter but also their skills and confidence, thus fostering self-motivated and self-regulated learning.

- Along the same lines, there are various tools for digital storytelling. Storytelling can be focused on a specific topic, or it can provide an opportunity for sharing personal, imaginary, or historical events. When storytelling, children engage with organising, evaluating, communicating and transforming learning and life experience in their own voices (Liu et al., 2011). Digital storytelling allows learners to incorporate text, images, photographs, audio and video files, as well as other artefacts, music and narration. The affordances of digital technologies can make this form of expression and learning more interactive, immersive and even personal, one that can be created and, most importantly, shared outside a particular classroom or setting. Examples related to this can be found in Chapter 4.

- In terms of sharing learning, the capabilities and connectivity of tools and devices such as tablets, iPads, and e-book readers, allow the immersion of young children in learning experiences that involve new forms of representation that can be interactive, illustrative and developmentally appropriate for introducing them to new learning endeavours (Gee, 2010). For example, adopting a participatory learning framework, Liu et al. (2013) explored the use of electronic book readers in collaborative storytelling. The reading experiences young children were introduced to were based on premises and practices of collaborative learning scaffolded by adult engagement. They were designed to elicit dialogic reading strategies, shared within reading communities. They conclude that socialised learning settings where 'collaborative experiences are made public on the web, allowing the viewing by peers ... [are] expected to motivate children to participate ... [while] the integration of multimedia components such as voice narrations and drawings could help parents elicit effective prompts to facilitate children to read' (Liu et al., 2013: 134–136).

- Digital technologies and the internet can be utilised to provide virtual simulations of real-life experiences. Examples of this constitute online and virtual museums, exhibits, points of interest, nature reserves and real-time journeys. These potentially highly immersive and interactive experiences are well suited for very young learners, and can be used as stimuli for interdisciplinary school projects that can cross the borders of an individual community or country. Facilitated by digital technologies, learning is personalised and can follow individual interests and motivations. Moreover, it can engage learners in real-world issues which can lead to authentic problem solving learning experiences linked to curricula.

- As follows from the above, formal and informal learning takes place through these experiences facilitated by digital technologies. Such learning engagements build on enquiry-based participatory learning environments that support critical thinking. They offer opportunities for linking learner engagement to curriculum content, blurring the line between formal and informal learning.

While not referring to specific tools, platforms, apps or devices by name, it is apparent that digital technologies and their affordances provide play and learning opportunities for negotiating shared understanding and values in global communities at an early age. It is argued that learning, working and living in a digital era creates the need for but also supports a set of skills that is moving from individual expression towards community involvement, where children, supported by adults and peers, negotiate their learning, their identity, role and citizenship in global networked communities and cultures of learners. This set of skills includes, but is not limited to, collaborative problem solving, multitasking, collective intelligence, the ability to search, evaluate and synthesise information, as well as that of negotiation in the sense of experiencing, discerning and respecting diverse communities, cultures and perspectives (Jenkins et al., 2009).

New challenges?

It has been supported that the characteristics and affordances of new digital technologies, even though conditional, can aid children's cognitive, social and emotional development, and support their self-efficacy and academic achievement (e.g. Hung et al., 2014). For example, game-based learning can provide virtual experiences in participatory learning environments that are user-centred and contain elements of fantasy and challenge. Such experiences can attract young learners' interest, increase their motivation and promote problem solving strategies, cooperation and collaboration (Gros, 2007), as well as foster peer and social interactions and skills (e.g. Janisse et al., 2014; Turkay et al., 2014), where learning can be experienced as a function of being part of a community's culture (Barab et al., 2000).

Sitting alongside this is the conflicting evidence on the possible negative outcomes that have been attributed to passive and overuse of technologies and media, such as child obesity, negative impacts on language and cognitive development, and behavioural and socio-emotional problems (e.g. Tomopoulos et al., 2010). This line of argument also highlights how learning and play experiences of younger children with technologies including e-books and tablets can potentially reduce the level of complexity present in children's imaginative non-technological learning and play, or that excessive use of animation could actually inhibit children's understanding of the text (e.g. Smirnova, 2011).

Among other challenges commonly noted in relation to digital technologies are: the fast-paced development of some of these technologies, devices, tools and apps; access and resource challenges and the associated costs – which also links to digital inequalities and more widely digital (il)literacy; early years professionals' and pedagogues' training needs and preparation required to use these technologies effectively in learning settings; difficulties in accessing or applying evidence-informed best practice; and the challenges that can arise when linking digitally infused learning to the objectives addressed by curricula and current educational policy.

This almost inevitably leads us to the conclusion that what is important is the meaning that children attribute to their experiences with new technologies, and how educators, pedagogues, parents and communities use these to support children's learning and development. For instance, with regard to game-based play and learning, despite their benefits, as discussed earlier, their potential to engage children in rich, authentic, meaningful, collaborative and culturally situated learning experiences is only possible if they are embedded in developmentally appropriate and culturally meaningful models of pedagogy and associated practice.

SUMMARY

In an era where advances in internet and communication technologies continue to be rapid, learning, working and living are continuously transformed. While the digital technologies that surround us cultivate diverse learning opportunities in a range of formal and informal learning contexts, it is important to remember that one size does not fit all. Technologies are often associated with increasing demands placed upon children and educators and, despite the emerging body of research and literature in this area, new questions continue to be generated about learning processes, experiences and contexts. What John Dewey (1907) supported over a century ago, that 'the child is already intensely active, and the question of education is the question of taking hold of his activities, of giving them direction', is still relevant. In other words, what is key here is not a focus on the technological tools alone, but rather how these are effectively embedded in early learning experiences.

There is a continuous demand for pedagogically sound theories and frameworks and evidence-based practices that can inform contemporary pedagogues and communities of learners. These can be used to guide us through learning and teaching approaches that aim to improve learning experiences, whatever form these take in a digital era. Reaching an understanding of effective pedagogies that can bridge the different forms of learning taking place around us with a range of different curricula involves thorough consideration of the different ways and processes in which children learn, and their alignment with authentic, meaningful, socially and culturally relevant communities of practice that digital technologies can nurture.

References and further reading

Anderson, T., and Whitelock, D. (2004) The Educational Semantic Web: Visioning and Practicing the Future of Education. *Journal of Interactive Media in Education*, 1: 1–15.

Barab, S.A., Squire, K. and Dueber, B. (2000) Supporting authenticity through participatory learning. *Educational Technology Research and Development* 48(2): 37–62.

Brown, J.S. and Adler, R.P. (2008) Minds on fire: Open education, the long tail and learning 2.0. *Educause Review* 43(1): 16–32.

Brown, J.S., Collins, A. and Duguid, P. (1989) Situated cognition and the culture of learning. *Educational Researcher* 18(1): 32–42.

Bulfin, S., Johnson, N.F. and Bigum, C. (2015) *Critical Perspectives on Technology and Education.* Basingstoke: Palgrave Macmillan.

Craft, A. (2012) Childhood in a digital age: Creative challenges for educational futures. *London Review of Education* 10(2): 173–190.

Davies, C., Coleman, J. and Livingstone, S. (2014) *Digital Technologies in the Lives of Young People.* Abingdon: Routledge.

Dewey, J. (1907) *The School and Society; Being Three Lectures, Supplemented by a Statement of the University Elementary School.* Chicago, IL: The University of Chicago

Press. Retrieved from: https://archive.org/stream/theschoolandsoci00deweuoft/the schoolandsoci00deweuoft_djvu.txt (accessed 28 January 2017).

Dewey, J. (1915) *The School and Society.* Chicago, IL: University of Chicago Press.

Duffy, T.M. and Cunningham, D. (1996) Constructivism: Implications for the design and delivery of instruction. In D. Jonnasen (ed.), *Handbook of Research for Educational Communications and Technology.* Mahwah, NJ: Lawrence Erlbaum, pp. 170–198.

Fischer, G. and Konomi, S. (2007) Innovative socio-technical environments in support of distributed intelligence and lifelong learning. *Journal of Computer Assisted Learning* 23(4): 338–350.

Fuchs, C. (2010) Social software and Web 2.0: Their sociological foundations and implications. In S. Murugesan (eds), *Handbook of Research on Web 2.0, 3.0, and X.0: Technologies, Business, and Social Applications.* New York: Information Science Reference, pp. 764–789.

Gee, J.P. (2010) *New Digital Media and Learning as an Emerging Area and 'Worked Examples' as One Way Forward.* Cambridge, MA: The MIT Press.

Gros, B. (2007) Digital games in education. *Journal of Research on Technology in Education* 40(1): 23–38.

Hedges H. and Cullen, J. (2012) Participatory learning theories: A framework for early childhood pedagogy. *Early Child Development and Care* 182(7): 921–940.

Hung, C., Huang, I. and Hwang, G.J. (2014) Effects of digital game-based learning on students' self-efficacy, motivation, anxiety, and achievements in learning mathematics. *Journal of Computers in Education* 1(2): 151–156.

Janisse, H.C., Bhavnagri, N., Li, X., et al. (2014) Impact of classroom computer availability on preschoolers' social interactions. *NHSA Dialog: A Research-to-Practice Journal for the Early Intervention Field* 17(3): 16–34.

Jenkins, H., Purushotma, R., Weigel, M., et al. (2009) *Confronting the Challenges of Participatory Culture: Media Education for the 21st Century.* Cambridge, MA: The MIT Press.

Lave, J. and Wenger, E. (1991) *Situated Learning: Legitimate Peripheral Participation.* Cambridge: University of Cambridge Press.

Liu, C.-C., Chen, H.S.L., Shih, J.-L., et al. (2011) An enhanced concept map approach to improving children's storytelling ability. *Computers and Education* 56(3): 873–884.

Liu, C.-C., Tseng, K.-H. and Wu, L.-Y. (2013) A participatory learning framework for enhancing children's reading experience with electronic book readers. *Research and Practice in Technology Enhanced Learning* 8(1): 129–151.

Mayes, T. and de Freitas, S. (2004) *Review of E-Learning Theories, Frameworks and Models.* London: Joint Information Systems Committee.

McLoughlin, C. and Lee, M.J.W. (2007) Social software and participatory learning: Extending pedagogical choices with technology affordances in the Web 2.0 era. In R. Atkinson and C. McBeath (eds), *ICT: Providing Choices for Learners and Learning. Proceedings of the 24th ASCILITE Conference,* Singapore: Proceedings ascilite, 2–5 December, pp. 664–675.

Morris, R.D. (2011) Web 3.0: Implications for Online Learning. *TechTrends* 55(1): 42–46.

Paavola, S., Lipponen, L. and Hakkarainen, K. (2004) Models of innovative knowledge communities and three metaphors of learning. *Review of Educational Research* 74(4): 557–576.

Papert, S. (1991) Situating constructionism. In I. Harel and S. Papert (eds), *Constructionism.* Norwood, NJ: Ablex, pp. 1–11.

Smirnova, E.O. (2011) Psychological and educational evaluation of toys in Moscow Center of Play and Toys. *Psychological Science and Education* 2: 5–10.

Tomopoulos, S., Dreyer, B.P., Berkule, S., et al. (2010) Infant media exposure and toddler development. *Archives of Pediatrics and Adolescent Medicine* 164(12): 1105–1111.

Turkay, S., Hoffman, D., Kinzer, C.K., et al. (2014) Toward understanding the potential of games for learning: Learning theory, game design characteristics, and situating video games in classrooms. *Computers in the Schools: Interdisciplinary Journal of Practice, Theory, and Applied Research* 31(1–2): 2–22.

Wenger, E. (1998) *Communities of Practice: Learning, Meaning, and Identity.* Cambridge: Cambridge University Press.

Wood, D.J., Bruner, J.S. and Ross, G. (1976) The role of tutoring in problem solving. *Journal of Child Psychiatry and Psychology* 17(2): 89–100.

3

RE-IMAGINING PLAY WITH NEW TECHNOLOGIES

Nicola Yelland and Caja Gilbert

CHAPTER OVERVIEW

It has become increasingly apparent that young children use new technologies in their daily lives and that they are fluent in their use. The work of Marsh (e.g. Marsh et al., 2005) and Plowman and colleagues (e.g. Plowman and Stephen, 2005) and the various surveys of the use of new technologies (e.g. Commonsense Media, 2013; Livingstone and Haddon, 2011; Rideout et al., 2010) have clearly shown that young children use and enjoy a wide range of technologies. Yet, research also shows that children are maintaining their use of traditional materials, such a books, blocks and dolls (e.g. Rideout et al., 2010). This chapter considers the ways in which tablet technologies enable playful explorations (Yelland, 2011) as part of a multimodal childhood (exploring interests and concepts on different platforms and using different resources, both traditional and technological).

This chapter seeks to:

- Demonstrate the importance of, and challenge associated with, selecting appropriate technological resources to support playful explorations.
- Provide case study examples of the ways in which tablet computers can be utilised as part of multimodal playful explorations.
- Consider the pedagogical and curricular considerations in incorporating tablets for playful explorations within the Australian educational context.

One of the characteristics of 21st-century learning that distinguishes it from previous times, is that it is multimodal (Yelland, 2007; 2011). Young learners are able to explore concepts in a range of modalities and use different forms of representations to express their ideas. Examples from popular culture would be that they have watched television and become friends with Elmo (*Sesame Street*) and Dora the Explorer in two dimensions. They are also able to interact with Elmo and Dora 'dolls' in three dimensions and read about them in both traditional and e-books. They can play with apps on tablets and smartphones that incorporate their favourite characters (like Dora and Elmo) and create artworks with them using paints, crayons and a range of other materials. Learning in this way means that their concepts about 'Elmo' and 'Dora' are richer and more varied than they would have been without the experiences incorporating new technologies.

KEY DEFINITION

Multimodal learning

The opportunity to explore concepts from multiple modalities and to represent them in a variety of dimensions.

Yelland has previously advocated for consideration of 'technology as play' (Yelland, 1999) and conceptualised 'playful explorations' (Yelland, 2011). Playful explorations encapsulate new learning scenarios in the 21st century. Playful explorations enable young children to explore ideas using different modalities and representations so that they are able to understand and explore concepts in new and dynamic ways. The role of new technologies in this learning is significant. Yelland (2011: 11) has stated:

> ... playful explorations that are supported by new media and interactions with adults/practitioners provide contexts for dynamic opportunities for teaching and learning in the early years. One important consideration regarding the learning of young children has become apparent. We need to provide contexts so that young children are exposed to different modes of representations which in turn afford them the opportunity to formulate new understandings about their world and make meanings about ideas and concepts on the basis of their experiences.

But it is not enough just to say that playful explorations simply broaden the concept of play. New technologies extend play to include them in the repertoire of play experiences, but additionally those working with children have a role to scaffold learning so that it is articulated and represented by the children in a variety of modes. As Yelland (2011: 8) stated:

> In this way playful explorations provide evidence of children's multimodal learning and encourage the use of a variety of media and resources that are part of this learning as well as being artifacts of the learning process. This requires a rethinking of the literacy that is required as a basic skill to a new conceptualization of multiliteracies which are fundamental to social and personal futures for all citizens.

This chapter presents and discusses playful explorations in the context of learning scenarios that were observed in an early years educational context (with young children 3–4 years of age). Using data from an ongoing four-year project with young children and tablet technologies, the chapter provides empirical examples of young children playing with these technologies and explores the ways in which these learning situations afford contexts for new learning in the 21st century. This chapter specifically focuses on case study data from an early years class (3–4 years of age) in a large Australian city. Despite representing the Australian context for learning, the key message from this chapter – that play in the digital era has become multimodal – is relevant to early years practice internationally. It considers the question: *In what ways can tablet technologies support multimodal play and learning?*

Trial and error: Selecting 'appropriate' tablets to encourage playful exploration

Learning opportunities for children are shaped by pedagogical considerations made by practitioners. These considerations include appropriate selection of resources. With the rapid evolution in technological developments, consideration of appropriate resources for use by young children is vital in both research and practice. In this section, we offer some insights into how the selection of tablets can shape children's playful explorations as well as how technology use can be scaffolded and planned for within early learning experiences.

In the study which informs this chapter, the centres were originally provided with eight Asus Vivo tablets. These were not regarded as being ideal. They had seven-inch screens and a small, thin stylus. The staff working with children observed that due to the size of some of the students' fingers and their emergent fine motor skills, the move to the larger Microsoft Surface Pro II with a pencil-sized pen was beneficial. This was explained by one practitioner:

> Many students are struggling with control over the size of the working screen space [referring to the Asus device]. Developmentally most early years students are still working in large motor format and use large sweeping motions rather than fine motor. Furthermore children at this age tend to anchor a piece of paper, or in this case the device, with their opposite hand. This means that for some children part of the screen is obscured. (Practitioner A)

The tablets provided an opportunity for practitioners to investigate whether the bigger screen size and easier to access buttons would support learning for younger children who were still developing their fine motor skills. The eight tablets were originally placed on a table in the educational establishment's rooms, just like any other activity planned by the practitioners (e.g. collage, drawing, threading). However, after a while, one of the practitioners thought that it would be more effective to incorporate them into the programme by having them integrated into the various planned activities. So, for example, a Surface was added to a 'Post Office' play area as part of the props (Figure 3.1), while another was used at the 'learning about numbers' play table (Figure 3.2) so that the children could participate in number activities on the apps that included games as well as creating numerals with the pen.

Figure 3.1   Using the tablet in the 'Post Office' play area

Figure 3.2   Learning about numbers with the tablet

Additionally, the devices could be taken outside into the playground where the camera was often used. The practitioners were initially concerned about the tablets being dropped, or getting dirty or wet if they were used outside in the playground. However, their views changed as they came to realise the durability of the tablet and the learning benefits that accrued as a result of using it outside to document play and to facilitate environmental investigations. For more information about outdoor play with technologies, see Johnston and Highfield's discussion in Chapter 5.

Using the tablet in classrooms in this way provided contexts for deep learning and the application of 21st-century skills (Fullan, 2013; Fullan and Langworthy, 2014) in a variety of ways, which will be shown in this chapter. The case studies illustrate the ways students are able to engage and be creative, using critical thinking skills, while collaborating and communicating their ideas to an audience. These essential elements of 21st-century schooling are enacted in the context of curriculum frameworks, which support knowledge creation as well as the exploration of existing knowledge.

Playful explorations with technologies: Case study examples

Children are able to incorporate technologies into their play in a variety of ways and for various learning opportunities. In this section, we describe how children used technologies to engage in:

- Creative or artistic play.
- Self-reflection and documentation.
- Storytelling and creation.

These experiences represent only a small sample of the ways in which technologies can be used to facilitate multimodal playful explorations. Yet they begin to give an insight into contemporary and digital childhoods. They present tablet technologies as another tool for learning, which needs to be pedagogically framed appropriately by practitioners. This theme is extended in the remaining chapters in the book.

CASE STUDY 1   CREATIVE AND ARTISTIC PLAY

The opportunity to create art electronically gave the children the chance to play with different media for drawing and encounter multimodal representations. The students enjoyed using the pen to create electronic artwork, including drawing figures (Figure 3.3). They also enjoyed using their fingers directly on the screen to create abstract pieces and loved to experiment with all the inbuilt features (stamps, magic paintbrushes) that they could find in the apps. The students discussed their art with whoever was near them at the time, explaining why they preferred one drawing to another, or highlighting the differences between the two formats. These are valuable early literacy moments that give children the opportunity to build their vocabulary as they become more confident about articulating their ideas orally when asked to explain what they have drawn using the different materials.

Multimodality was also a feature of a self-portrait drawing session (Figure 3.4). The children observed their face in a mirror and then drew themselves both in pencil and using an app on the tablet called Tux Paint.

Figure 3.3   Using a painting app   **Figure 3.4**   Creating self-portraits
on the tablet

CASE STUDY 2   SELF-REFLECTION AND DOCUMENTATION

The children also used the tablets to take photos of themselves and each other while they were playing, usually outside (Figure 3.5). One of the practitioners noted:

... they were outside in the play area and they had the Surface outside and they were actually photographing each other at play. And then I was fascinated because I was watching the kids and it was so interchangeable! They were using their fingers for the big sweeping motions that they needed and then picking up the stylus for the intricate aspects of what they were doing. So they were just interchanging. The seamless interchange between finger and stylus, finger, stylus. (Practitioner B)

From a pedagogical perspective, this use of technology links closely with well-established approaches to early years provisions, such as Reggio Emilia. In addition, we can see the autonomy associated with children's learning by facilitating children to document their own learning.

Figure 3.5   Taking photos during outdoor play

CASE STUDY 3   STORY CREATION

Using the Kids Story Builder app, students were able to create digital stories by choosing photos, adding text and audio to tell their story. This was an exciting time and the practitioners showed much interest in pursuing this sequence of events since it related to the children not only being creative in terms of photography, but also gave them opportunities to become autonomous in deciding what they recorded as being of interest to them, and having a permanent record of this which could be shared with parents and reflected upon at any time (please see Figures 3.8a–d for an example).

Learning in the 21st century: Pedagogical and curricular considerations

Since the advent of tablet technologies in 2010, with the launch of the (Apple) iPad, it has become evident that the mobility and convenience of the tablets has made them extremely useful in the early years with young children, who can use them both spontaneously and effectively in much more diverse contexts than previous types of new technologies. The learning scenarios from the case studies presented in this chapter reflect young children's learning using the 21st-century skills as a frame for discussion. The tablets were used in a play-based early childhood programme which was guided by the principles inherent to the Early Years Learning Framework (EYLF) (DEEWR, 2009) and we worked with the practitioners to encourage playful explorations (Yelland, 2011) as they encountered a variety of experiences during their time in and out of the classroom.

In Australia, the Federal government took a major initiative in early childhood education with their release of the EYLF (DEEWR, 2009). The document provided a vision for children's learning that considered both pedagogies and learning outcomes, and this was the first time that this had been formulated at the national level. The title and theme of the framework was *Belonging, Being and Becoming*, with the goal that all children should be able to 'experience learning that is engaging and that will build success for life' (DEEWR, 2009: 7). Five learning outcomes were identified. They were that children should:

- Have a strong sense of identity.
- Be connected with and contribute to their world.
- Have a strong sense of wellbeing.
- Be confident and involved learners.
- Be effective communicators.

The role of information and communication technologies (ICT) was simply stated under learning outcome 5, where it said that children would use information and communication technologies to 'access information, investigate their ideas and represent their thinking' (2009: 4). The vision for learning in the early years as exemplified in the EYLF was documented as being able to assist early childhood practitioners to create their own (local) learning opportunities relevant to their programme within a broader context of the first years of early education. It was designed to act as a guide for curriculum decision making, planning, implementing, evaluating and to communicate young children's learning to their parents. It promoted play as the main context for learning on the basis that it:

- Allows for the expression of personality and uniqueness.
- Enhances dispositions such as curiosity and creativity.
- Enables children to make connections between prior experiences and new learning.
- Assists children to develop relationships and concepts.
- Stimulates a sense of wellbeing.

While these features map to the overall vision stated in the five learning outcomes they are also compatible with other considerations for learning in the 21st century that have moved away from a view of curriculum as content to the acquisition of 21st-century skills (Partnerships for the 21st Century, 2008). There were originally four of these skills: creativity, critical thinking, collaborating and communicating (Trilling and Fadel, 2009), but they have since been extended to include citizenship and character education (Fullan, 2012). Further, it was also recognised that fluency with new technologies was regarded as an essential component of future employment across a range of opportunities and had a role to play in early childhood programmes (Cuban, 2001). Here, we describe three of the elements critical thinking, collaboration and communication, since creativity was included in the first case study above, and in fact permeates all the activities that were experienced by the children. Similarly, the ongoing tasks of building character and citizenship are inculcated in the pedagogical work of teachers on a continuing basis and form part of the 'hidden curriculum' (Zorec and Dosler, 2016).

Critical thinking

There were a number of apps available to the students on the Surface. Two of the most popular were a memory game, Animals Memory 2, and the School Writing app (free to all Australian schools) that helped them to practise drawing numerals and letters (Figure 3.6). The use of the stylus/pen was useful for this activity since it enabled the children to form the numerals and letters accurately with the device rather than always use their fingers. Thus, it allowed students to develop dexterity with the pen that would not have been possible if they had drawn the figures with their fingers. The use of apps focused on skill building with young children has been shown to be valuable in terms of providing them with the opportunity to use skills in an enjoyable context (Yelland and Gilbert, 2013, 2014). It also encouraged and facilitated critical thinking about scenes and using their literacy and numeracy skills as they encounter them in an engaging modality.

Using the camera also afforded the opportunity to introduce early mathematical language like positional and relational terms (Yelland et al., 2014) so important for early numeracy activities. For example, when the children were in the playground they might be located on top of the ladder, or digging in the sandpit, or sitting on a block (Figure 3.7).

The class was also involved in watching both chickens and plants grow. One practitioner described the process:

> So we've been taking photos of the chickens every day and we're going to make a book out of it. We have the chickens for two weeks and then the children get to take them home. We'll have [the book ready] by the end. So what happens is the chickens will hatch and then after they hatch they stay the same size for a little while so we won't need to do a page every day, so by the end of it we'll have the book all ready. We've got the interactive whiteboard, so we'll be able to put it on there when it's done. We'll do it together. They'll tell me what to write, rather than me just writing it. So I'll show them the picture and they'll tell me what's happening in the pictures. They love the recording of their voices too. [We're using] Kid's Story Builder. (Practitioner A)

Engaging the children in collaborations is vital for this age group and creating a shared book (Figures 3.8a–d) is a relevant and exciting way to make early reading connect with their lives and interests. In one class they documented their planting of seeds in an e-book that could be read by individuals or small groups of children. But as the practitioner noted, because they also had an interactive whiteboard, they could use it as a whole group shared reading activity. In this way the children are able to communicate their ideas and findings to a larger audience.

Figure 3.6   Forming numerals using School Writing on the tablet

Figure 3.7   Relational and positional terms can be learnt taking photographs during outdoors play

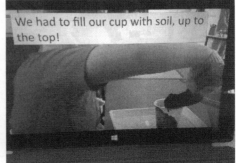

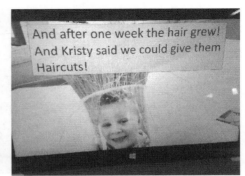

Figures 3.8a–d   Children created a digital account of growing grass

Collaborations

Attending kindergarten is often the first time that 4-year-olds encounter other children of the same age and it provides a context for social encounters and developing social skills, like sharing and collaborating with others, especially around shared resources such as the device. The collaborative e-books and taking photographs, described previously, are examples of activities that required the children to collaborate with each other with specific desired learning outcomes. The practitioners also indicated that they felt that having the tablets encouraged the children to share and take turns. It was evident in the observations that the children were able to take turns with the devices, for example, when playing in the 'Post Office' play area. Additionally, they waited for their turn to take photos with the camera when outside.

Communication

The communication of ideas and shared reading of e-books were the most popular uses of the tablets. The class even used them in their daily yoga sessions with the practitioner to know precisely how they should be doing their moves the right way. One of the main benefits was that the practitioner was able to show and share the work of the children with their parents. At this age, there were limitations on communicating to a broader audience and peer-to-peer communication, but it was evident that the creation of e-books around the topics of 'living things' enabled the children to talk to each other about their experiences, while having the interactive whiteboard also facilitated talking and sharing with the whole group.

SUMMARY

The kindergarten group were on the first step of their formal education journey. The school has a vision to 'have a cohort of students who are responsible global citizens and we want them to be able to make decisions based on how that decision affects more than just the local context' (Practitioner B). Having tablets as a resource for their learning encouraged them to encounter and use 21st-century skills in play-based contexts that are engaging and linked to their lived experiences. One practitioner said that she 'noticed different strengths come out of the children when they're using the tablets'. Engagement is an integral part of deep learning. The examples of this group of young children not only revealed their high levels of engagement with ideas, but also provided contexts in which they could encounter, use and practise 21st-century skills and build their capacity in literacy and numeracy in multimodal formats that can be built on as they progress through the schooling system.

Feedback from the practitioners also indicated that they used the tablets as a teaching device when they were discussing a topic in group time since they were able to support questioning and reflections:

We've used them in a couple of group times. So if we're talking about a subject, instead of getting a laptop out we'll just go on the Internet so that they can see something. Like we were talking about circus tents and they wanted to know what a real circus tent looked like, so we looked up what it was on the Surface. The practitioners could use the Surface Pen to highlight key information identifying and discussing characteristics. (Practitioner A)

The data provided here illustrate the seamless ways in which new technologies and traditional materials can be mixed and incorporated into various play scenarios to constitute effective multimodal learning contexts. These have included adding specific technologies to traditional learning scenarios, like creating a post office, as well as providing new opportunities for creating technological representations, such as in drawing a personal portrait. Living and learning in the 21st century enables us to use technological as well as traditional materials and resources for our lived experiences and problem solving. We should be eager to take advantage of them in order to make sure that all young children are engaged in optimal learning opportunities to ensure their futures.

Useful website

www.weareteachers.com/16-apps-that-will-motivate-even-your-most-resistant-readers-2

References and further reading

Bird, J. and Edwards, S. (2014) Children learning to use technologies through play: A digital play framework. *British Journal of Educational Technology* 46(6): 1131–1191.

Commonsense Media (2013) *Zero to Eight: Children's Media Use in America 2013*. Retrieved from: www.commonsensemedia.org/research/zero-to-eight-childrens-media-use-in-america-2013# (accessed 27 January 2017).

Cuban, L. (2001) *Oversold and Underused: Computers in the Classroom*. Cambridge, MA: Harvard University Press.

DEEWR (Department of Education, Employment and Workplace Relations) (2009) *Belonging, Being and Becoming: The Early Years Learning Framework*. Canberra: Commonwealth of Australia.

Fullan, M. (2012) *Great to Excellent: Launching the Next Stage of Ontario's Education Agenda*. Toronto: OISE.

Fullan, M. (2013) *Stratosphere: Integrating Technology, Pedagogy and Change Knowledge*. Toronto: Pearson.

Fullan, M. and Langworthy, M. (2014) *A Rich Seam: How New Pedagogies Find Deep Learning*. ISTE.

Garvis, S. and Lemon, N. (eds) (2015) *Understanding Digital Technologies and Young Children*. Abingdon: Routledge.

Livingstone, S. and Haddon, L. (2011) *EU Kids Online*. London: London School of Economics. Retrieved from: www.lse.ac.uk/media@lse/research/EUKidsOnline/EU%20 Kids%20I%20%282006-9%29/EU%20Kids%20Online%20I%20Reports/EUKids OnlineFinalReport.pdf (accessed 27 January 2017).

Lynch, J. and Redpath, T. (2014) 'Smart' technologies in early years literacy education: A meta-narrative of paradigmatic tensions in iPad use in an Australian preparatory classroom. *Journal of Early Childhood Literacy* 14(2): 147–174.

Marsh, J.A., Brooks, G., Hughes, J., et al. (2005) *Digital Beginnings: Young Children's Use of Popular Culture, Media and New Technologies*. Sheffield: Literacy Research Centre, University of Sheffield. Retrieved from: www.digitalbeginnings.shef.ac.uk/Digital BeginningsReport.pdf (accessed 27 January 2017).

Partnerships for the 21st Century (2008) *21st Century Skills, Education and Competitiveness: A Resource and Policy Guide*. Washington, DC: The Partnership for 21st Century Skills.

Plowman, L. and Stephen, C. (2005) Children, play, and computers in pre-school education. *British Journal of Educational Technology* 36(2): 145–157.

Rideout, V.J., Foehr, V.J. and Roberts, D.F. (2010) *Generation M2: Media in the Lives of 8 to 18 Year-Olds*. Menlo Park, CA: Kaiser Family Foundation Study. Retrieved from: http://kff.org/other/poll-finding/report-generation-m2-media-in-the-lives (accessed 27 January 2017).

Shifflet, R., Toledo, C. and Mattoon, C. (2012) A preschool practitioner's story. *Young Children* 67(3): 36–41.

Trilling, B. and C. Fadel (2009) *21st Century Skills: Learning for Life in our Times*. San Francisco, CA: Jossey-Bass.

Yelland, N.J. (1999) Technology as play. *Early Childhood Education Journal* 26(4): 217–220.

Yelland, N.J. (2007) *Shift to the Future: Rethinking Learning with New Technologies in Education*. New York: Routledge.

Yelland, N.J. (2011) Reconceptualising play and learning in the lives of children. *Australasian Journal of Early Childhood* 36(2): 4–12.

Yelland, N.J. and Gilbert, C.L. (2013) *iPlay, iLearn, iGrow*. Research report presented to IBM. Retrieved from: www.ipadsforeducation.vic.edu.au/userfiles/files/IBM%20 Report%20iPlay,%20iLearn%20%26%20iGrow.pdf (accessed 27 January 2017).

Yelland, N.J., Diezmann, C. and Butler, D. (2014) *Early Mathematical Explorations* (2nd edition). Melbourne: Cambridge University Press.

Yelland, N.J. and Gilbert, C.L. (2014) *SmartStart: Creating New Contexts for Learning in the 21st Century*. Research report presented to IBM. Retrieved from: www.ipadsfor education.vic.edu.au/userfiles/files/226543%20Vic%20Uni%20IBM%20Report%20 Smart%20Start%202.pdf (accessed 27 January 2017).

Zorec, M.B. and Dosler, A.J. (2016) Rethinking the hidden curriculum: Daily routine in Slovenian preschools. *European Early Childhood Education Journal* 24(1), 103–114.

PART 2
CHILDREN'S TECHNOLOGICAL EXPERIENCES

4

CREATIVE AND DRAMATIC PLAY WITH TECHNOLOGIES

Lorna Arnott, Pauline Duncan and Deirdre Grogan

CHAPTER OVERVIEW

Creativity and technology shape not only the educational landscape in the Western 21st century but also the workforce, industry and society overall. Early years provision is a driving force, within education, in the adoption of both technology and creative processes. Play and free-choice time allow both practitioners and children to engage creatively with technological resources. This chapter will explore creative play with technologies in early childhood contexts in two ways:

- Examples of observed episodes of creativity with digital technologies, technological toys and broadly defined technological resources will be presented.
- Consideration will be given to the affordances of the technologies and the learning context and how these both contribute to the creative play of children.

Throughout this chapter, we seek to describe how play-based experiences are fundamental to facilitating creative play with technologies.

In an increasingly global economy, driven not only by knowledge but also innovation, creativity is taking centre stage (Green and Hannon, 2007). Society has progressed from the focus on industry as the cornerstone to success, through information and knowledge economies and is now firmly invested in the creative economy. Creative thinking and production are now considered paramount (Resnick, 2008). Indeed, creativity is considered one of the key skills required for adaptation and success in this fast-paced and changing workforce (Craft, 2003; Wheeler et al., 2002). It is deemed a determinant of economic growth.

The prioritisation of creativity reflects the continued and profound interest in technologies in society. Technologies are informing our work, learning and leisure times.

The dependence on technologies is so great that recent psychological work suggests that some individuals are being diagnosed with nomophobia – separation anxiety when not connected and contactable (King et al., 2013). Technologies are being designed to increase efficiency and productivity and so investments in technologies are extensive and research around technology in education and life is prolific.

Technology and creativity therefore form two strands of a global agenda, but in reality they work in tandem with creativity driving innovative technologies, which in turn provide new possibilities and encourage new ways of thinking, therefore fuelling creativity. The creative and technological relationship is a cyclical and reciprocal one; they are interdependent. Society and education are therefore steered towards a techno-creative path.

In education specifically, it is essential to understand the synergy between creativity and technologies. It has been recognised that schools and education have a key role to play in shaping the creative economy (Green and Hannon, 2007). As a result, there are an increasing number of policy statements relating to the inclusion of creativity in school and early years curricula (Craft, 2003, 2012). Learners are continually being encouraged to be creative thinkers (Claxton, 2007), and teachers encouraged to nurture student creativity (Fischman et al., 2006).

This chapter seeks to explore this timely synergy in the early years education context by describing children's creative play experiences with technologies. It will draw on data from research projects about children's creativity and social play. This research evidence allows us to present case studies of four different episodes of creative play with technology and offers examples of the role of technologies when openly integrated into play opportunities. We conclude by discussing how the affordances of the technologies and the learning context shape children's creative play.

What is creativity and creative play with technologies

Like technology, definitions of creativity are universally challenged and debated. Howard-Jones et al. (2002), for example, talk about creativity in terms of producing 'appropriate' and 'original' 'solutions'. Others like Saracho (1992) discuss creativity as a process. Thus, several typologies, frameworks and models of creativity are available in the literature with their own nuanced differences. In this chapter we explore creativity as a process in order to link this clearly with play experiences.

KEY DEFINITION

Creativity

Prentice (2000: 145) explains that 'creativity is a complex and slippery concept. It has multiple meanings, and for anyone writing about creativity in an educational context it is necessary at the outset to acknowledge that an established, precise and universally accepted definition does not exist'.

A focus on play is essential to this discussion, particularly, as Hoffmann and Russ (2012: 175) explain that, 'Creativity and play are naturally connected, as a child uses fantasy, symbolism, and divergent thinking to weave a context, story, and characters.' Similarly, Saracho (2002: 435) suggests that 'play provides a domain for creative expression and the encouragement of the creative processes'. Children's ability to play and their level of playfulness is therefore considered to create dispositions for creativity throughout life (Howard-Jones et al., 2002). Yet little is known about how the creative play processes are being transformed, if at all, in light of the digital and technological resources available.

This is an important area to explore, particularly as research shows that technologies are now readily available to children at younger ages (Palaiologou, 2016a) and because commercial organisations are marketing many toys as 'creative' in order to articulate their educational appeal to parents. Research evidence that links creativity with specific toys and resources, let alone technological toys, is relatively limited in availability and we therefore need a better understanding of how children use these resources in a creative way. This chapter begins to unpick this link between creative play and toys, focusing specifically on technological toys.

Across the research projects that inform this chapter, it was clear that four distinct episodes of creative play took place when children use technology. Throughout the next section we illustrate how children engaged with technologies in creative ways, including: through storytelling; as props in pretend play; as construction tools where building and design was the foundation; and by using technologies in unconventional ways. A case study is presented for each episode of creative play. The findings are valuable, particularly in light of evidence from practice which suggested that 'digital devices are not seen as offering such opportunities and are viewed as static and controlling children's creativity, motivation and exploration' (Palaiologou, 2016b: 315). The case studies informed the following section, where we discuss the role of the affordances of the technology as well as the environment or context in shaping children's creative play.

Episodes of creative play with technology

Throughout this section we frame creative play through four possible episodes and offer a brief link between these case studies, theory and literature in each episode.

Episode 1: Storytelling and technology

With the increase in user-friendly tablet software, creative play can be facilitated through digital storytelling. Robin (2008: 222) suggests that:

> ... digital storytelling allows computer users to become creative storytellers through the traditional processes of selecting a topic, conducting some research, writing a script, and developing an interesting story. This material is then combined with various types of multimedia, including computer-based graphics, recorded audio, computer-generated text, video clips, and music so that it can be played on a computer, uploaded on a web site, or burned on a DVD.

We categorise digital storytelling as an episode of creative play because of the clear link between the cognitive structures which are inherent in children's play but that are also fundamental to creative thinking. For example divergent thinking – the ability to consider many possible answers or approaches – is fundamental to both play and to creativity. Storytelling is another element which is both creative and playful, particularly when we think of it as a performance as described by Baas et al. (2008).

During storytelling we are able to gain an insight into the children's imagination and fantasy abilities. For digital storytelling in early years contexts, this would require careful 'scaffolding' (Wood et al., 1976) by practitioners or parents, including skilful selection of appropriate media software which is accessible to children. Case Study 1 demonstrates how this may be framed and planned in an early years context where engagement and understanding of the process are central to encouraging children's participation and therefore facilitating their creativity. While the example presented is a simple recording system, this approach offers great possibilities for young children's creativity.

CASE STUDY 1   STORYTELLING

Figure 4.1   The 'video-booth'

Elsewhere, we have indicated that technologies, particularly tablet computers like iPads, offer young children a medium to articulate their creativity (Arnott et al., 2016). During this same project, one such mechanism used for expression was storytelling with the aid of puppets that was recorded on the iPad and used for discussion and reflection. The model used in our project was open-ended with children selecting any puppets desired and creating an unscripted story to camera, offering a very free-flowing and ad hoc story. We created an engaging 'video-booth' with draped fabrics, props, puppets and a children's sofa, to allow children to record their stories (Figure 4.1).

The children involved in our study enjoyed being able to use the puppets to 'tell their story'. The puppets provided a voice or character to guide the storytelling process. It allowed children to have a 'face' for their story if they did not want to tell the story as themselves. The video-booth created an engaging space which gave the storytelling an exclusive feel and children were able to use the space independently, with peers or alongside a practitioner or adult.

Episode 2: Technology as a prop in pretend play

Pretend play is considered a key opportunity for creativity and in driving the creative process, particularly because of the significant involvement of fantasy and symbolism (Russ, 2003). 'As early as infancy children utilize their imagination, drama, and narrative when they become exceptionally absorbed in a fantasy world' (Saracho, 2002: 435). Thus, as we alluded to in previous sections, there is a strong link between so many of the cognitive and affective (emotional) processes involved in creativity and those in play (Russ, 2003). Saracho (2002) goes as far as to say that pretend play 'cultivates' those processes. The wealth of evidence which documents the link between traditional pretend play and creativity is comprehensive.

Fewer studies have begun to explore pretend play with technologies and so the link between this kind of play and creativity in a technological context is less understood. One of the challenges associated with technology in education, and often one of the reasons that technologies are criticised in early childhood, is the limited and narrow definition of technology employed. For example, often the deficit model of technology which criticises technologies for being socially and cognitively detrimental focuses on screen-based media and overlooks the wealth of other technological resources available in children's early life and learning. For this reason, playing in clusters or with peers in general was not often explored in relation to technologies. Instead, the focus was on the 'children-at-computer' as Wang and Ching (2003) point out. By adopting a broader definition of technology, as presented in Chapter 1, we are able to see overwhelming amounts of evidence that children incorporate technologies into their pretend play, in much the same way that they use traditional technologies. For example, elsewhere Arnott (2016) describes how children use technologies to act out a Chinese restaurant. This kind of play is also clearly evident in Chapter 8 on play with working and non-working technologies.

The following case study describes how children used technologies as part of a broader pretend play theme of running a bank, linking to high levels of imagination and fantasy. In these situations, the technologies become a prop in the pretend play, rather than the central activity in the way that a computer game may guide the play.

CASE STUDY 2   PRETEND PLAY WITH TECHNOLOGY

Several children are using an electronic shopping till and pretending to use the till to run a bank. They all have various amounts of money and some children have plastic credit cards. Children continually visit the child who is controlling the till and request money to be withdrawn from their accounts. For example, Andy sits to the side of John and says '£10 please'. John hands him a bank note. Andy says 'thank you' and pretends to walk away. Later, John swipes the credit card then presses buttons and numbers appear on the screen (3555). John says '£50' really loud. Andy returns and hands a bank note to John and says '£50'. John hands him change and Andy leaves. Children are quite confident in the play theme with these technologies as David (another boy waiting in the queue), while waving a plastic credit card, turns to the researchers who are observing and explains 'it's a bank.' The play continues with children engaged for an extended period.

Episode 3: Technological construction and design

Construction resources are a standard 'creative' toy and are marketed as such by commercial producers. It is believed that practical application fosters creative abilities (Wheeler et al., 2002). In contemporary childhood, construction resources have progressed from simple LEGO bricks or Froebel Blocks towards a multifunctional array of motorised and robotic resources. These may include Motorised Meccano, LEGO Technics and Mindstorms as well as Gears Gears Gears cog construction sets. With these sets children are able to create ever more elaborate and often 'working' (in terms of motion, light and sound) constructions.

While the main aim of these resources is to facilitate creative play, there has been much debate over the contemporary marketing of such resources and whether this is stifling creativity. The concern now is that 'design packs' are being created with the exact number and make-up of resources required to create, for example, a helicopter or hairdressing salon. Children are therefore building to design briefs rather than using imagination and creative thinking. This is a problem, considering that 'children's imaginativeness is a dimension of creativity' (Saracho, 2002: 435).

We witnessed such challenges when we observed children using motorised construction resources in our study (demonstrated in Case Study 3), whereby children followed instructions to complete the 'task'. While this is not a negative experience and links to increased problem solving and logical processing, it does detract somewhat from the notion of 'possibility thinking' and the 'what if' approach to construction (Burnard et al., 2006). We attribute this stifled approach to a lack of familiarity with the resources and insufficient time to play with the resources to extend the play beyond an initial exploration phase. With familiarity comes greater confidence to experiment and stray from the design template. If time allowed greater familiarity with the resources, we anticipate that episodes of divergent thinking may still have been possible. This draws our attention to the importance of investigating the context around which technologies are used and how insufficient it is to explore technologies as isolated objects devoid of *context*.

CASE STUDY 3   TECHNOLOGICAL CONSTRUCTION FOR CREATIVITY

Anna is playing with motorised construction resources. She works hard trying to join the square pieces together. Her and her mum look at the box cover for the resource and discuss it. She finds a manual and says 'look here's the instructions'. She looks at the instructions again and turns the pages. She watches as Mum tries to attach the wheel to the motor. She looks around and mum says, 'what do you want to make?' Anna points to the manual and says 'I'm looking for that thing'. She finds it and says 'ah'. Anna says, 'Nana Nana can you help me make a roundabout [on the cover of the box]?' Gran replies 'ok'. Gran then helps Anna use the manual to construct something. They look at the book and gather the pieces that they need to use. They continue to look for pieces for a long time.

Episode 4: Using technologies in unconventional ways

Divergent thinking is central to creativity because of the link with generating ideas to solve a problem. It involves a particular set of skills such as fluidity of thinking, which is strongly linked to creative ability (Russ, 2003). Play is one mechanism where children are able to practise these process and this is particularly obvious when children use toys and objects in different forms and representations. We are able to see objects used in a playful and symbolic manner where they are transformed by the child (Hoffmann and Russ, 2012). This is one of the cornerstones of traditional pretend play activities.

By utilising the broader definitions of technologies put forward in this book, we can see episodes of such divergent thinking and transformation of technological objects in much the same way as children do with traditional resources. In traditional play resources we see curved Froebel Blocks being transformed into a gun because the curve creates a handle to hold, or we are all familiar with the classic Vygotskian description of a child transforming a stick into a horse. With technologies we see an electronic shopping till (cash register) becoming a bank teller's computer (as in Case Study 2), or a Meccano remote controlled car kit may become a doctor's kit (Arnott, 2016).

Here we are able to unpick the role that the 'technological affordances' (Carr, 2000) have in shaping children's perceptions of what these technologies can become and ultimately children's creative play. This is further demonstrated in Case Study 4.

CASE STUDY 4   TRANSFORMING TOYS AND OBJECTS

Linda is playing with pieces from the motorised cogs game as well as the remote controlled Meccano set. She carried two wheels and the remote control and gives this to her mum and says, 'It's a car'. She picks up a round piece from the motorised cogs game and says, 'I am driving – driving in my car.' She shouts, 'I've stopped!

(Continued)

(Continued)

The car will get me to park – there in no air in my car.' Mum asks if she wants 'air' and Linda collects the Meccano remote control and pretends to fill her car wheels with air by tipping the remote control up and attaching the cable from the remote to her car wheels. She stops again, 'I've no petrol!' She then repeats the motion with the Meccano remote control to put petrol in her car. Then, 'I've stopped again, no wheels.'

Technological affordances and technological contexts for creative play

The aforementioned episodes of creative play demonstrate how technologies, when used in a playful way and integrated into early years pedagogies as 'tools' rather than distinct and different objects (Arnott, 2016), can provide opportunities for creativity. It is undeniable that to some extend the affordances of the technology contribute to how the technologies are used in creative play, just as they do with traditional resources. For example, the number of component parts to the resource may influence whether children collaborate or play independently (Savage, 2011).

One affordance which was particularly contributory to creative play was the level of challenge associated with the technological toy. The examples presented in Case Studies 1 and 3 describe how children needed support with the resources because of the level of challenge associated with the resource. When unsupported with the technological construction resources, some children remained within the exploratory phase of play rather than creating or building any original output or employing any imaginative thought with these resources. They were unable to understand how the resources worked or what they were designed to do.

In other instances, the perceived uses of the technology were interpreted easily by children. For example, the mechanics of these resources spurred interest as children repeatedly pressed the motor buttons to carefully analyse how the resource operated and then, after understanding the functions of the technologies, were able to integrate the resources into their creative play. For example, one child built a road out of Froebel Blocks to walk their motorised toy, treating the robot like a pet with the attached cable and remote control acting as the leash for the pet. In this episode, because the resource 'walked' and because it had a remote control attached, the child was able to assimilate their knowledge of the robot resource with their understanding of walking a pet on a leash and then was able to create the appropriate environment (a road) to do so. Here we begin to see what Pellegrini (1984) distinguishes between exploration and play. Children start with the 'what is it?' question before moving on to asking 'what can I do with it?'. With these resources (motorised gears), this level of creativity would be further extended when the child has the confidence to reconfigure the robot into different types of pets, or moveable toys rather than creating a play scene around its current form. Here we would begin to see what Burnard et al. (2006) describe as 'possibility thinking'.

Yet the affordances of the resource in isolation does not determine how technologies are used in creative play. Saracho (2002: 436) suggests that 'classroom environments can either cultivate or stifle creativity and the likelihood to achieve innovation'. When the notion of 'environment' is interpreted in the broadest sense, to also include social and cultural elements, our data clearly demonstrated that other people, such as parents, peers or teachers, also shaped children's creativity, often more so than the affordance of the resource. For example, the data extract below demonstrates how a parent working with a child encouraged them to engage in 'easier' play, which in turn potentially stifled their creative development.

Data extract 1 (family playing with Gears Gears Gears construction toys)

Emma looks at the funfair box and stares at the picture.

Emma points at the picture and says to Dad 'what we need to do is make the same as this OK?'

Dad responds by saying 'that will take too long, too many bits'.

Emma seems displeased and says 'come on'.

Dad points out the stickers that are lying on the table close by and offers them as an alternative and says 'what about the stickers there?'

Emma looks at the stickers and starts to hand them out. 'Mum you can have a shiny one.' She walks over to Mum and hands her a sticker. Mum replies, 'thanks very much.'

She looks at the technology box and says 'we can make a ...' but Dad interrupts and says 'what about the big blocks over there?'

Thus, we are seeing more and more 'creative technologies' such as 'computer-based programs and equipment that are not pre-prepared or constructed ...[that] allow students to design, build and program with as little or as much support as is needed' (McDonald and Howell, 2012: 642) being developed. The resources, however, are only one part of the puzzle in early years education. We need to continually consider the framing of technological activities and how these can be integrated and supported as part of a play-based pedagogy if we wish to foster children's creative play. Data from our research suggest that when framed in an open and play-based manner children are highly creative in their integration of technological tools and resources. Creative play and pretend play are inextricably linked and, much like non-technological toys, technologies are utilised by children as props in their play scenes. We need to recognise these resources as contemporary tools that represent modern living, rather than as pre-defined activities or games with narrowly defined parameters or outcomes. To foster children's creative play we need to think creatively about how we integrate technologies into early childhood experiences.

SUMMARY

Throughout this chapter we have demonstrated the essential link between play and technology in order to facilitate creative play. We have illustrated how, when using a broader definition, technologies can be integrated into play-based pedagogies and from this creative play can emerge. Here we have presented four episodes of children's creative play with technology: storytelling, using technologies as props in pretend play, technological construction and design and utilising technologies in unconventional ways. This is not an exhaustive list but rather offers an insight into the multitude of ways that we can extend our use of technologies as tools in our play to facilitate creative experiences with children. We must not consider technologies to be squarely defined resources with fixed attributes that are un-mouldable, instead we must use our own creativity to facilitate creative play with children and technology.

References and further reading

Arnott, L. (2016) The role of digital technologies. In I. Palaiologou (ed.), *Early Years Foundation Stage: Theory and Practice*, 3rd edn. London: Sage, pp. 329–342.

Arnott, L., Grogan, D. and Duncan, P. (2016) Lessons from using iPads to understand young children's creativity. *Contemporary Issues in Early Childhood* 17(2): 157–173.

Baas, M., De Dreu, C.K. and Nijstad, B.A. (2008) A meta-analysis of 25 years of mood-creativity research: Hedonic tone, activation, or regulatory focus? *Psychological Bulletin* 134(6): 779–806.

Burnard, P., Craft, A., Cremin, T., et al. (2006) Documenting 'possibility thinking': A journey of collaborative enquiry. *International Journal of Early Years Education* 14(3): 243–262.

Carr, M. (2000) Technological affordance, social practice and learning narratives in an early childhood setting. *International Journal of Technology and Design Education* 10(1): 61–80.

Claxton, G. (2007) Expanding young people's capacity to learn. *British Journal of Educational Studies* 55(2): 115–134.

Craft, A. (2003) The limits to creativity in education: Dilemmas for the educator. *British Journal of Educational Studies* 51(2): 113–127.

Craft, A. (2012) Childhood in a digital age: Creative challenges for educational futures. *London Review of Education* 10(2): 173–190.

Fischman, W., DiBara, J.A. and Gardner, H. (2006) Creating good education against the odds. *Cambridge Journal of Education* 36(3): 383–398.

Green, H. and Hannon, C. (2007) Their space: Education for a digital generation, DEMOS. Retrieved from: http://dera.ioe.ac.uk/23215 (accessed 27 January 2017).

Hoffmann, J. and Russ, S. (2012) Pretend play, creativity, and emotion regulation in children. *Psychology of Aesthetics, Creativity, and the Arts* 6(2): 175–185.

Howard-Jones, P., Taylor, J. and Sutton, L. (2002) The effect of play on the creativity of young children during subsequent activity. *Early Child Development and Care* 172(4): 323–328.

King, A.L.S., Valença, A.M., Silva, A.C.O., et al. (2013) Nomophobia: Dependency on virtual environments or social phobia? *Computers in Human Behavior* 29: 140–144.

McDonald, S. and Howell, J. (2012) Watching, creating and achieving: Creative technologies as a conduit for learning in the early years. *British Journal of Educational Technology* 43(4): 641–651.

Palaiologou, I. (2016a) Children under five and digital technologies: Implications for early years pedagogy. *European Early Childhood Education Research Journal*, 24(1): 5–24.

Palaiologou, I. (2016b) Teachers' dispositions towards the role of digital devices in play-based pedagogy in early childhood education. *Early Years* 36(3): 305–321.

Pellegrini, A.D. (1984) The effects of exploration and play on young children's associative fluency: A review and extension of training studies. In T.D. Yawkey and A.D. Pellegrini (eds), *Child's Play: Developmental and Applied*. Hillsdale, NJ: Erlbaum, pp. 237–253.

Prentice, R. (2000) Creativity: A reaffirmation of its place in early childhood education. *The Curriculum Journal* 11(2): 145–158.

Resnick, M. (2008) Sowing the seeds for a more creative society. *Learning and Leading with Technology* 35(4): 18–22.

Robin, B.R. (2008) Digital storytelling: A powerful technology tool for the 21st century classroom. *Theory into Practice* 47(3): 220–228.

Russ, S.W. (2003) Play and creativity: Developmental issues. *Scandinavian Journal of Educational Research* 47(3): 291–303.

Saracho, O.N. (1992) Preschool children's cognitive style and play and implications for creativity. *Creativity Research Journal* 5(1): 35–47.

Saracho, O. (2002) Young children's creativity and pretend play. *Early Child Development and Care* 172(5): 431–438.

Savage, L. (2011) *Exploring Young Children's Social Interactions in Technology-Rich Early Years Environments*. Stirling: University of Stirling, Institute of Education.

Wang, X.C. and Ching, C. (2003) Social construction of computer experience in a first-grade classroom: Social processes and mediating artifacts. *Early Education and Development* 14(3): 335–362.

Wheeler, S., Waite, S.J. and Bromfield, C. (2002) Promoting creative thinking through the use of ICT. *Journal of Computer Assisted Learning* 18(3): 367–378.

Wood, D., Bruner, J.S. and Ross, G. (1976) The role of tutoring in problem solving. *Journal of Child Psychology and Psychiatry* 17(2): 89–100.

5

TECHNOLOGY IN OUTDOOR PLAY

Kelly Johnston and Kate Highfield

CHAPTER OVERVIEW

For many children technology is an increasingly common, easily accessible part of their everyday lives (Nikolopoulou and Gialamas, 2015). Children have a dynamic relationship with the various contexts with which they interact, including family, early learning settings and the wider community (DEEWR, 2009; Rogoff, 1990) and as such it stands to reason that technology should be incorporated into early learning settings in a way that mirrors the experiences children have within their family environments, as well as their wider social contexts. This requires a broader conceptualisation of digital technologies and consideration of how these can be used to support authentic play-based learning across contexts. This chapter argues that technology needs to be reconceptualised as a resource to facilitate and support play, and that outdoor play and technology should not be dichotomised. Children, practitioners and parents need to understand the various forms of technology that will continue to feature throughout children's lives. Similarly, children need to experience nature and engage in exploration and play outdoors. Adopting a broad definition of technology allows us to marry these two fundamental components of contemporary children's play. Within this chapter technology is defined and conceptualised as: anything that can create, store or process data – this could include digital toys or other devices such as computers or tablets (Palaiologou, 2016); less tangible forms of technology such as the internet (Knight and Hunter, 2013); and imaginary technologies – such as those that appear in dramatic play (Edwards, 2014; Howard et al., 2012).

The chapter explores three key issues in relation to technology and outdoor play in early childhood:

- Outdoor play with technologies should be viewed as a mechanism for children to have increased autonomy and agency in their learning experiences.
- There is a false dichotomy when we consider technology as a structured indoor experience, whereas outdoor play is often viewed as 'free play'.
- Conceptualisations of technology need to move beyond the passive screen media lens – in relation to outdoor experiences this could include digital resources such as a GPS, compass, microscope or camera/video.

Technology has a central place in play-based curricula across the world, for example in the the Early Years Learning Framework (EYLF) in Australia and the Curriculum for Excellence in Scotland. The EYLF is a document guiding teaching and learning in Australian preschool contexts, and defines early childhood curricula as: 'all the interactions, experiences, activities, routines and events, planned and unplanned, that occur in an environment designed to foster children's learning and development' (DEEWR, 2009: 9).

These curricula reflect children's experiences and social contexts, and involve both indoor and outdoor environments. Reconceptualising the use of technology involves moving past viewing it as the main focus of an experience – for example, children using a computer with software that focuses on numeracy or literacy games. Instead, integrating technology as an everyday tool or resource can present a valuable means for consolidating and extending on children's experiences with technology as well as fostering an awareness of how things work in the 21st century (Parette et al., 2010). This can only be achieved if we consider technologies which move beyond screen-based media to be used as part of our practice.

Outdoor play and technology: A mechanism for autonomy

The value of encouraging children to reconnect with nature and to spend more time engaged in outdoor play is a common theme in early childhood education. The EYLF (DEEWR, 2009) includes a strong focus on promoting outdoor education as well as natural materials and resources:

> Outdoor learning spaces are a feature of Australian learning environments. They offer a vast array of possibilities not available indoors. Play spaces in natural environments include plants, trees, edible gardens, sand, rocks, mud, water and other elements from nature. These spaces invite open-ended interactions, spontaneity, risk-taking, exploration, discovery and connection with nature. They foster an appreciation of the natural environment, develop environmental awareness and provide a platform for ongoing environmental education. (DEEWR, 2009: 15–16)

Similarly, across the world we see similar appreciation for the benefits of outdoor play for children, resulting in increasing numbers of full-time outdoor kindergartens in Scandinavian countries as well as in the UK. Outdoor environments are often seen as a realm in which children can engage in more child-led, open-ended play (Maynard, 2014), but it is important to distinguish between this as 'free-play' and not 'free-reign' (Touhill, 2013). Educators recognise that outdoor play provides many opportunities for independence and autonomy and as such provides a valuable platform for intentional teaching. Pivotal to the opportunities afforded through outdoor play is agency – where children have the ability to instigate and follow their own investigations, to create their own play scenarios and ultimately feel a 'sense of control, empowerment or agency' (White and Woolley, 2014: 35).

Given the already challenging arena of outdoor play for young children and the similarly challenging focus on technologies in early years, a pivotal consideration here is whether, and how, there is a place for technology to support children's explorations, discoveries and connections outdoors. The risk with our considerations of technology in the outdoor environment is that we will limit our focus to passive technology or consumptive technologies. Here educators can accidently fall into the false dichotomy of technology as an indoor activity, contrasting it to 'free play'. In reality, however, the outdoor environment often provides children with specific and significant autonomy. In this regard, it is very similar to technology use, which, given the connectivity associated with these resources, also offers children opportunities for increased autonomy and exploration, when managed correctly. This chapter provides such examples of how technologies can effectively be integrated into children's outdoor play experiences in order to offer increased autonomy and agency in the play process.

The false dichotomy of outdoor play and technology

Current research suggests understandings of technology within children's play need to be reconceptualised to reflect children's experiences with technology and the skills they will need as they develop as digital citizens (Edwards, 2014). Despite the recognition of the ubiquity of technology in children's lives, there remains a resistance to integrating technology into play-based early learning curricula (Palaiologou, 2016). Additionally, technology use in early childhood has predominantly been defined within the narrow parameters of computer use (Stephen, 2013), which has relegated it largely to the confines of indoors. An important progression has been the reconceptualisation of technology to reflect children's contemporary experiences. This can encompass an ever growing range of digital media, including television, computers, gaming consoles, DVD players, smartphones, high-tech toys, iPods, touchscreen tablets and household appliances (Fleer, 2011; Palaiologou, 2016). These resources are often 'blamed' for challenging behaviour or social isolation among young children. Yet Louv (2010: 137) suggests that:

> The problem with computers isn't computers – they're just the tools; the problem is that overdependence on them displaces other sources of education, from the arts to nature.

As has been highlighted in the Introduction to this book, due to the ubiquitous nature of technology, debates around whether technology should or should not feature in early childhood programmes are no longer at the forefront. Instead, discussion and reflection are beginning to focus on the types of technology for inclusion and how these resources are integrated into the curriculum.

Extending on these definitions, this chapter discusses the benefits of interactive technologies such as digital microscopes, video recording devices, programmable toys and cameras to extend on children's explorations and investigations in the outdoors as part of their play-based learning.

It is important not only to discuss definitions and conceptualisations of technology as a resource in play, but also to ensure that we have a clear understanding of what play is, and why it is such an integral and central feature in preschool curricula. The value of play in supporting early childhood learning and development is widely recognised in research and literature (Siraj-Blatchford, 2009; Sumsion et al., 2014), and subsequently underpins early childhood education in many contexts, including Australia. The EYLF (DEEWR, 2009), Australia's mandatory national framework that guides practice in all preschool settings, notes:

> [Play-based learning is] a context for learning through which children organise and make sense of their social worlds, as they engage actively with people, objects and representations. (DEEWR, 2009: 6)

Extending on this statement, Siraj-Blatchford (2009) notes that when engaging in play children are not just copying what they already know, they are unpacking and organising information in their journey of understanding their world. While play by its very nature needs to be child-led and directed, it is further supported and facilitated when linked with intentional teaching (Sumsion et al., 2014). In this way children's play maintains the key attributes of joy and autonomy, while also being relevant to their previous experiences, interests and ways of knowing the world (Shifflet et al., 2012). This has significant implications when considering authentic and effective integration of technology into early childhood curricula. It leads us to ask a number of questions, such as: What does this mean for play and learning that takes place outdoors? Is this different from play and learning indoors? And are there certain tools and resources that should only be used in these particular contexts?

Moving beyond the screen: Examples of outdoor play with technology

The case studies presented in this chapter illustrate how technology can be effectively integrated into outdoor play to further enhance children's experiences, working contemporaneously and in a complementary manner with a number of other non-digital tools and resources. They also present findings of children driving the use of technology, actively engaging with it to collaboratively and individually test ideas and theories, and to enrich their outdoor play and learning experiences.

Louv's (2010) work on outdoor experiences for children speaks of a 'broken bond between children and nature' (p. 163) and notes that educators can help to repair this disconnect. There is no denying the value of children engaging with nature in a way that is meaningful, authentic and ongoing. Similarly, there is no denying the prevalence of technology and its often-pervasive presence in everyday life. However, when we consider the difference between active and passive engagement with technology it is possible to consider ways that technology can be considered as an everyday resource, to extend learning and play in outdoor contexts.

Case studies 1 and 2

Case studies 1 and 2 are examples of practice gathered during a larger doctoral research project investigating educator beliefs and practices in integrating technology in preschool settings in Australia. Here, children's engagement is observed in the setting or recounted by educators during interviews, and supported by secondary data such as written/visual documentation of the experiences.

CASE STUDY 1   DOCUMENTING AND OBSERVING WITH TECHNOLOGY

At an Australian preschool setting children (4–5 years of age) were engaged in an ongoing experience in alignment with World Environment Day. Educators were observed taking photographs throughout the day. It appeared to be an accepted, everyday occurrence and digital images were mainly utilised for documentation and planning purposes. Documentation within the room reflected an additional purpose and provided insights into how photography was used to support children's thinking. One example showed children working together to plant new plants in their garden in association with World Environment Day. The educator took video footage of the children digging, planting and watering, and then sat with the children as they watched the footage. Digital photographs and children's drawings were also included in the display to document the experience. In the following days, the children viewed the documentation of their activities, including digital photographs and videos. The children not only commented on what they were doing, but also had discussions over what their peers were doing during the experience.

This vignette highlights a different view of outdoor play-based learning. Through the inclusion of digital recordings children were able to see the perspectives of others – something they were not able to do when initially engaged in the experience as they were primarily focused on their own tasks. Use of this technology ultimately helped them to gain a broader understanding of the whole experience. This activity provides a strong example of children engaging with and experiencing nature, yet using technology as an integrated tool to support and extend on their investigations, explorations and interactions. Such an approach aligns with Rinaldi's (2006) reflections on learning in Reggio Emilia:

> In the Reggio classroom, digital tools are not isolated from non-digital tools as in a computer lab; rather, they are available among other tools in the classroom environments and used within larger projects. (p. 139)

Within the larger outdoor-based project described in this vignette the digital tools helped children to develop a sense of identity to support them to learn how to develop relationships with others and to respond to them with respect, understanding and acceptance, as well as creating a sense of community. Technology was able to provide an additional resource for reflection, supplementing other resources and providing a medium through which children could discuss and reflect on their shared experiences relating to gardening and the environment.

For these children, seeing themselves and their work in digital displays was a normal integrated part of everyday learning and reflection. Digital documentation was a valuable way for children to revisit, further investigate and extend on their learning and experiences. The decision to include these various forms of technology was based on children's interests and reactions to it. As one educator at the service noted:

> [Technology is] just so much easier. The kids actually respond to it, like a big part of it. They really do.

Children's familiarity with these forms of digital devices had positioned them as cultural tools within the children's worlds (Vygotsky, 1986). Children had assimilated a knowledge of these resources as a culturally significant tool and assimilated them into their explorations and investigations. Additionally, providing children with the opportunity to document the experience afforded them an additional level of agency as the person behind the camera holds the power in choosing what is important and what is worth documenting (Flannery Quinn and Manning, 2013). When children themselves are able to document their experiences it further contributes to their agency and control in play situations – two traits already synonymous with outdoor play (Touhill, 2013). Additionally, technology in the form of digital documentation was deemed an effective and appropriate medium for extending children's understanding, without altering or redefining their play. This ultimately contributed to a curriculum that reflected various elements promoted in the EYLF such as responding to children's interests and ways of being, promoting cultural competence and supporting children in their developing sense of identity (DEEWR, 2009). This process also links clearly to well-established methods of early years provision across the world, such as Reggio Emilia (Katz, 1998).

CASE STUDY 2   TECHNOLOGY AS A TOOL

At an Australian preschool setting a class of children (3–4 years of age) and their educators began exploring roots as part of an ongoing investigation into plants and gardening. During an interview an educator commented:

> So now we started a digging patch outside with the children. ... So we found worms and treasures and different things, rocks and looked at them. We found roots as well but those roots are quite stuck in the ground, in the soil, so we couldn't get them out. But it's something [the children] don't know yet, they are called roots, so we looked at them. We got different answers from different children.

> They don't know yet they are roots and I haven't told them so it's going to be a journey to discover together what are those roots – what are those things we found in the garden called? So I'm intending to use technology in this way – The Internet ... we might get samples of the root and have them under the microscope and look at them. Get some books and look at the books and compare ...

> I'm thinking later on, after we discover they are roots we [can] talk about the root vegetables that we eat. ... Talk about carrots, beetroot and all these things so we incorporate technology in that as well.

At this preschool setting, educators viewed technology as a tool to support and extend children's learning and investigations in both indoor and outdoor play experiences. One of the key purposes of using digital resources was to encourage children to ask questions, and to support them in testing their theories and hypotheses and in extending their ideas – factors which are identified as contributing to effective outdoor learning environments (White and Woolley, 2014). Digital resources were used to extend on and complement more traditional resources such as reference books and information posters and were also able to provide an additional level of information.

Initially, children were asked to share their observations of the roots, and were then supported to use a digital microscope to gain further insights – or to collect additional data. Importantly, the educator took time to introduce the new form of technology being used. She asked the children what they thought the device was and then she specifically named the tool and explained what it did, using authentic language such as 'optical instrument'. The children then took turns using the microscope with the educator helping them to adjust it.

In Case Study 2 technology was not used to simply provide answers. Children were encouraged to hypothesise as to what plant the roots belonged to, and to share ideas and discuss possibilities before then using books and internet searches to test some of their theories. Here technology was integrated as a meaningful tool rather than the main focus of the activity or stand-alone experience. This is similar to the concept of convergence outlined by Edwards (2015), which acknowledges it is difficult to separate technology in children's play from the more traditional resources due to the inter-relations and inter-reliance that exist between them. Edwards (2015) is referring to the links between digital technologies and popular culture in children's play, but parallels can be seen with the examples in this case study where technologies (both tangible, such as computers, and intangible, such as using internet searches) and traditional resources such as reference books are used to supplement and support each other. With outdoor play acknowledged for its potential to support agency and autonomy, is it important to consider technology as another tool through which children can develop critical thinking skills, explore, theorise, communicate and express their understandings.

Case Studies 3 and 4 arise from a larger research project. Within these projects teachers have shared their concerns and successes with young children's use of technology.

CASE STUDY 3   CONSUMING TECHNOLOGY

Sarah was an experienced educator working within a school in a 'transition' class. This group of 4- and 5-year-olds were attending an excursion at the beach. The class, working in small groups and accompanied by parent helpers, were exploring the beach and rock pool areas. Sarah noticed one of her pupils sitting alone with his parent watching, as he avoided the planned exploration and instead played an app on his mother's phone. After redirecting the child to the appropriate task Sarah was surprised when the parent stated, 'Oh I thought it was OK – the game practised maths'.

CASE STUDY 4   CREATING WITH TECHNOLOGY

James (aged 6) was at the beach with his family, and noticed a 'Blue Bottle' (a small blue coloured jellyfish) on the beach. Using his mother's phone he and his sister (aged 3) took photos of the animal before returning to play. Later that night James showed his father the photos and asked questions about the sea creature. James then worked with his father to investigate Blue Bottles, exploring the varieties, their habitats and creating a collage (using an app called Pic Collage) of his images and information to share with his peers.

Case Studies 3 and 4 are provided to contrast two different uses of the technology. The first has a child playing a game, consuming premade content in the outdoor environment. Armstrong et al. (2015) suggest the ideas of *consuming* or *creating* with technology as a means to differentiate between the experiences. Within this frame passive media would be considered consuming media, with creative media including tools where a child can explore, investigate, create and communicate. Here the technology, or the parent allowing him to use the technology in this context, can be seen as a dissuasion or a distraction to outdoor play. In part, the rewarding nature of the technology and the child's response to this diminished his autonomy as a play creator and participant. Case Study 4, despite being in a similar beach context, shows the children using technology to capture their explorations and then to inspire research. The technology here acted as a facilitator, quickly capturing and documenting a discovery, for later investigation.

In both case studies the media mentor (here a teacher or parent) plays a key role in monitoring, assisting and reframing. For example James's investigations with his father in Case Study 4 could only happen with assistance and scaffolding. In a world where technology can be pervasive, the role of the adult here is key in modelling technology use in a way that maintains a child's autonomy in the play cycle.

SUMMARY

Throughout this chapter we have provided examples of how technology can be seen to support and extend children's experiences in outdoor play. This aims to create a discourse that challenges the bifurcation of technology and outdoor play by demonstrating that digital technology can support children's autonomy and agency in their learning experiences. To achieve this increase in understanding of the potential value of technology in outdoor play it is important for educators to continue to consider broad and diverse conceptualisations and definitions of technology – particularly beyond passive screen media.

Useful websites

Resources from Early Childhood Australia:
The digital business kit (www.earlychildhoodaustralia.org.au/our-work/digital-business-kit)
Learning modules (www.earlychildhoodaustralia.org.au/our-work/digital-business-kit/digital-business-kit-module-1)
Video collection (www.earlychildhoodaustralia.org.au/our-work/digital-business-kit/digital-business-kit-module-2)
Live Wires (www.earlychildhoodaustralia.org.au/our-work/digital-business-kit/live-wires)

References and further reading

Armstrong, A., Donohue, C. and Highfield, K. (2015) Technology integration: Defining what is appropriate for young children. *Exchange* 225(222): 28–33.
DEEWR (Department of Education, Employment and Workplace Relations) (2009) *Belonging, Being and Becoming: The Early Years Learning Framework for Australia.* Canberra: Commonwealth of Australia.
Dietze, B. and Kashin, D. (2013) Shifting views: Exploring potential for technology integration in early childhood education programs. *Canadian Journal of Learning and Technology* 39(4): 1–12.
Dwyer, N. and Highfield, K. (2015) Technology, our tool not our master. *Every Day Learning* 3(4): 1–28.
Edwards, S. (2014) Towards contemporary play: Sociocultural theory and the digital-consumerist context. *Journal of Early Childhood Research* 12(3): 219–233.

Edwards, S. (2015) New concepts of play and the problem of technology, digital media and popular-culture integration with play-based learning in early childhood education. *Technology, Pedagogy and Education* 25(4): 1–20.

Flannery Quinn, S.M. and Manning, J.P. (2013) Recognising the ethical implications of the use of photography in early childhood education settings. *Contemporary Issues in Early Childhood* 14(3): 270–278.

Fleer, M. (2011) Technologically constructed childhoods: Moving beyond a reproductive to a productive and critical view of curriculum development. *Australasian Journal of Early Childhood* 39(1): 16–24.

Howard, J., Miles, G. and Rees-Davies, L. (2012) Computer use within a play-based early years curriculum. *International Journal of Early Years Education* 20(2): 175–189.

Katz, L. (1998) What can we learn from Reggio Emilia? In C. Edwards, L. Gandini and G. Forman (eds), *The Hundred Languages of Children: The Reggio Emilia Approach – Advanced Reflections.* Greenwich, CT: Ablex, pp. 19–40.

Knight, K. and Hunter, C. (2013) *Using Technology in Service Delivery to Families, Children and Young People.* CFCA Paper No. 17. Australian Institute of Family Studies, Child Family Community Australia. Retrieved from: http://aifs.gov.au/cfca/pubs/papers/a145634/ (accessed 27 January 2017).

Louv, R. (2010) *Last Child in the Woods: Saving Our Children From Nature-Deficit Disorder.* London: Atlantic Books.

Maynard, T. (2014) Supporting 'child-initiated' activity in the outdoor environment. In T. Maynard and J. Waters (eds), *Exploring Outdoor Play in the Early Years.* Maidenhead: Open University Press, pp. 141–156.

National Association for Education of Young Children and the Fred Rogers Association for Early Learning and Children's Media at Saint Vincent's College (2012) *Technology and Interactive Media as Tools in Early Childhood Programs Serving Children from Birth Through Age 8.* Retrieved from: www.naeyc.org/files/naeyc/PS_technology_WEB.pdf (accessed 27 January 2017).

Nikolopoulou, K. and Gialamas, V. (2015) ICT and play in preschool: Early childhood teachers' belief and confidence. *International Journal of Early Years Education* 23(4): 409–425.

Palaiologou, I. (2016) Teachers' dispositions towards the role of digital devices in play-based pedagogy in early childhood education. *Early Years* 36(3): 305–321.

Parette, H. P. Quesenberry, A. C., and Blum, C. (2010) Missing the boat with technology usage in early childhood settings: A 21st century view of developmentally appropriate practice. *Early Childhood Education Journal* 37(5),: 335–343.

Rinaldi, C. (2006) In *Dialogue with Reggio Emilia: Listening, Researching and Learning.* Oxford: Routledge.

Rogoff, B. (1990) *Apprenticeship in Thinking: Cognitive Development in Social Context.* New York: Oxford University Press.

Shifflet, R., Toledo, C. and Mattoon, C. (2012) Touch tablet surprises: A preschool teacher's story. *Young Children* 67(3): 36–41.

Siraj-Blatchford, I. (2009) Conceptualising progression in the pedagogy of play and sustained shared thinking in early childhood education: A Vygotskian perspective. *Education and Child Psychology* 26(2): 77–89.

Stephen, C. (2013) Guided interaction: Exploring how adults can support children's learning with technology in preschool settings. *Hong Kong Journal of Early Childhood,* 12(1): 15–22.

Sumsion, J. Grieshaber, S., McArdle, F. and Shield, P. (2014) The 'state of play' in Australia: Early childhood educators and play-based learning. *Australasian Journal of Early Childhood* 39(3): 4–13.

Touhill, L. (2013) Promoting independence and agency. *National Quality Standard Professional Learning Program* 64. Retrieved from: www.earlychildhoodaustralia.org.au/nqsplp/wp-content/uploads/2013/10/NQS_PLP_E-Newsletter_No64.pdf (accessed 27 January 2017).

Vygotsky, L. (1986) *Thought and Language.* Massachusetts: The MIT Press.

White, J. and Woolley, H. (2014) What makes a good outdoor environment for young children? In T. Maynard and J. Waters (eds), *Exploring Outdoor Play in the Early Years.* Maidenhead: Open University Press, pp. 29–41.

Wyver, S. and Little, H. (2014) Outdoor play in Australia. In T. Maynard and J. Waters (eds), *Exploring Outdoor Play in the Early Years.* Maidenhead: Open University Press, pp. 141–156.

6

YOUNG CHILDREN DEVELOPING LITERACY AND NUMERACY SKILLS WITH TECHNOLOGY

Rachael Levy and Nathalie Sinclair

CHAPTER OVERVIEW

The purpose of this chapter is to explore how young children's engagement with literacy and numeracy can be developed through their interactions with digital technology. This chapter draws from a wide body of literature, and empirical data, to understand how technology facilitates young children's learning and reflect on what this means for children's engagement with literacy and numeracy today. With reference to studies that look specifically at the acquisition of literacy and numeracy skills and practices, we show how there is a wide research base indicating that technology affords opportunities for young children to engage with concepts and develop skills and practices in both of these areas. The second half of this chapter builds on this, by making reference to data gathered recently whereby 6-year-old children were engaged in using the maths application TouchCounts (Sinclair and Jackiw, 2014) on an iPad. Although TouchCounts is a maths application and has been designed to promote engagement with mathematical concepts, we demonstrate how it provides an opportunity for collaborative learning that involves a use of many skills including those pertaining to numeracy and literacy. Analysis of the data, taken from the perspective of the child, illuminates the importance of the adult in supporting children's learning within the context of the technology. Thus, the chapter seeks to:

- Describe the state of play in relation to technology and literacy in early years.
- Introduce the role of technologies in numeracy development.
- Present an overview of the role of the TouchCounts application for literacy and numeracy development.

Technology features in the lives of children from the moment they are born. Dubbed as a generation of 'Digital Natives' (Prensky, 2001a) and 'High Tech tots' (Berson and Berson, 2010), the literature makes clear that young children are growing up in environments that are rich in digital media (Hsin et al., 2014; Plowman et al., 2012). This 'technologisation of childhood' (Plowman et al., 2010) has given rise to the anxiety that aspects of childhood are now threatened by the proliferation of technology (Alliance for Childhood, 2004; Buckingham, 2000). Yet Plowman et al. (2010) not only make the point that parents generally do not perceive technology to be the threat that it is often portrayed, the majority of parents recognise a value in integrating technology into their children's lives, including infants and toddlers (Weber, 2006).

This value is undoubtedly connected with the concept of *learning*, leading to questions about the affordances of technology in the lives of young children and the ways in which learning is facilitated through interaction with digital media. It is well documented that schooled constructions of learning, which are reflected in standardised assessment procedures, may be in discord with home constructions; the role of digital technology is especially salient here as young children's engagement with digital texts can often go unrecognised within the school curriculum and its assessment (Levy, 2008, 2009). For this reason it appears that an initial step must be to recognise the complexity of the relationships between technology and learning. In order to do this, it becomes important to take a broad view of learning, that does not simply see achievement as something that is measured by standardised school-based assessment. Rather, this chapter takes the view that early childhood education is a space and place where children not only learn subject-specific content knowledge and skills, but learn how to engage with concepts, enhance their motivation for learning and essentially learn *how to learn*.

That said, much of what children are expected to learn, as they enter the formal education system, can be described as falling under the umbrella terms of 'literacy' and 'numeracy' (Manolitsis et al., 2013; Purpura et al., 2011). Given that a number of studies have indicated that exposure to literacy and numeracy concepts in the home supports children's future academic development in school (Duncan et al., 2007; LeFevre et al., 2009; Lukie et al., 2014), it is easy to see why so much concern is focused on literacy and numeracy in early childhood education. The purpose of this chapter is to explore how young children's engagement with literacy and numeracy can be developed through their interactions with digital technology. However, rather than trying to understand how technology can help children to meet standardised attainment goals, this chapter looks more broadly at the affordances of technology in encouraging engagement, motivation and confidence in literacy and numeracy, as well as acquisition of skills and knowledge.

This means that the chapter explores the relationship between technology and learning from the perspectives of the children themselves. As Hsin et al. (2014) indicate in their systematic literature review on empirical studies of how technologies influence young children's learning, much of this research has focused on collecting data from adults (i.e. parents or teachers). Moreover, they also point out that many of these studies were also concerned with understanding the adults' roles in children's use of technology. Yet as we have known for some time, 'the best source of information about issues pertinent to children is the children themselves' (Scott, 2000: 106).

In recent years, the inclusion of young children's voices in social and educational research has become increasingly evident. As Scott (2000: 98) argues, children are no longer regarded as 'incomplete adults', but as 'actors within their own right'; as a consequence researchers have recently developed 'a variety of strategies and tools to create pathways for young children's voices to be heard within research' (Levy and Thompson, 2015: 138). That is not to say that there is little value in data that have been collected from adults. For example, we have learned a great deal about the kinds of technologies children use in homes from studies that have surveyed and talked to adults (Marsh et al., 2005; Plowmen et al., 2012). However, the purpose of this chapter is to draw from a wide body of literature and empirical data to understand how technology facilitates young children's learning and reflect on what this means for children's engagement with literacy and numeracy today.

The first half of this chapter focuses on literacy and numeracy respectively; with reference to studies that look specifically at the acquisition of literacy and numeracy skills and practices, we show how there is a wide research base indicating that technology affords opportunities for young children to engage with concepts and develop skills and practices in both of these areas. The second half of this chapter builds on this, by making reference to data gathered recently whereby 6-year-old children were engaged in using the maths application TouchCounts (Sinclair and Jackiw, 2014) on an iPad. Analysis revealed that these children were not only developing mathematical knowledge and practices while using this application, but were also engaged in a wide variety of literacy skills. We demonstrate that technology such as iPads offers young children opportunities to interact with text and engage with concepts that may not always be possible within other media.

Technology and literacy

There is a vast and growing body of literature on technology and literacy, much of which supports the argument that young children use technology in ways that are innate and 'native' (Prensky, 2001a). For example, research has documented that 'very young children show expertise in on-screen reading, even where homes have no computers' (Bearne et al., 2007: 11), because interaction with such texts is now embodied within a culturally valued discourse. Moreover, further study has indicated that many young children develop skills and strategies within their home environments that allow them to access and read a variety of digital texts with fluency (Levy, 2009). In her study of 12 children aged 3–5, Levy discovered that these children were making sense of digital texts, and using them with independence, before they had begun their formal education. As they were drawing on their digital 'funds of knowledge' (Moll et al., 1992), they demonstrated an ability to make sense of print and image within the holistic context of multimodal reading.

Many other studies have shown that technology can promote children's ability to use literacy with confidence and independence. In a recent study of children from a nursery school, a reception class (ages 4–5) and a special school, Flewitt et al. (2015) discovered that iPads offered innovative opportunities for literacy learning; in particular children were seen to communicate effectively, collaborate with others and also develop their own independent learning. The teachers in the study reported that the iPads heightened children's concentration levels, which directly linked with increased motivation and independence. What is more, this had a direct impact on the ways in which some of the teachers in the study evaluated the literacy competence of the children with whom they were working. To illustrate, Flewitt et al. reported:

> Children's motivation to succeed in iPad activities sometimes led them to display more advanced literacy skills than staff had previously given them credit for. For example, the reception class teacher was 'blown away' by the quality of some children's iPad work, including those who were not keen on conventional writing activities. (2015: 299)

In addition, the literature also challenges the very notions of what *literacy* actually is, now that *text* has come to include screen-based as well as paper-based contexts. To take this further, Marsh and Singleton (2009: 1) point out that 'technology has always been part of literacy'. They go on to argue that in order to read or write, one needs to have certain tools (paper, pencil, computer screen, etc.), yet the 'nature of that technology inevitably influences the literacy experience' (Marsh and Singleton, 2009: 1). This assertion has led researchers to define literacy practices that are mediated by new technology, including text analysis and text production, as 'digital literacies' (Carrington and Robinson, 2009).

The concept of 'digital literacy' has been well debated in the literature, but while there are disagreements on how to formulate a definition of the term, there appears to be general agreement that digital literacy is not just about applying traditional constructions of reading and writing to the screen context. Merchant (2007) argues that digital literacy should be orientated towards the 'study of written or symbolic representation that is mediated by new technology'. Similarly, Marsh et al. (2005: 5) also acknowledges that 'there are distinct aspects of text analysis and production using new media' that cannot be described in the same way as the more traditional literacy practices.

KEY DEFINITION

Digital literacy

'Digital literacy' can help to 'redefine conceptualisations of literacy as an ability to understand the many sign and symbol systems in existence within texts today as well as the ways in which children make sense of them' (Levy, 2011: 152) within their home environments.

This suggests that while the construct of 'text' is becoming more complex and now includes multimodal (see Chapter 3 by Yelland and Gilbert) and screen texts, as well as paper-based modes, it is important to recognise that it is no longer appropriate to talk about the skills and practices of *reading* and *writing* in relation to paper-based media only. This was emphasised in a recent study by Wolfe and Flewitt (2010), who discovered that there were 'profound differences' in the ways that children used various modes when interacting with different technologies, including digital and traditional media. Wolfe and Flewitt concluded that as research into the ways in which children learn through the context of digital media is still relatively new, we are only just beginning to understand how children's literacy activity involving new technologies might be 'scaffolded'.

Miller and Warschauer (2014) agree that different media carry different affordances and that educators need to understand how children read and write within a variety of different contexts. Having reviewed research on e-reading, both in the pre-tablet and tablet era, they concluded that this difference needs to be embraced and accommodated by educators, stating:

> In sum, it appears based on this review of prior research that print-based resources and e-books are neither mutually exclusive, nor is technology a substitute for print. Rather traditional print books and e-books seem to play different roles in the literacy process, and eliminating this false dichotomy offers children more opportunity for diverse types of literacy experiences. (Miller and Warschauer, 2014: 294)

As these researchers point out, little is known about how children make sense of, and produce text within the context of, technology, yet research is beginning to identify some important factors. For example, in 2007 Bearne et al. reported the non-linear aspects of screen reading. More recently, Simpson et al. (2013: 123) built on this, showing that the affordances of touch technology allow for 'multimodal, multidirectional reading paths'. Having closely observed Grade 3 and Grade 5 children (ages 9–11) using iPads in the midst of literacy work, these researchers emphasised the importance of the role of touch in reading. They found that readers of different levels would equally partake in touch practices together and as a result, students of differing reading abilities were more inclined to work together through the context of the iPad rather than with print-based media. In addition, this study revealed that touch was linked directly to cognitive awareness. In reference to reading on the iPad, Simpson et al. (2013: 129) reported:

> Most of the actions demand typing, tapping, scrolling, and expanding texts and text components without explicitly emphasising the visual. More importantly from the perspective of sensory awareness, each touch needed to be employed at a specific velocity and appropriate level of pressure in order for the tablets to respond appropriately.

This led the researchers to conclude that when touch was enacted, meaning-making choices were made at 'physical and cognitive' (p. 129) levels. This is an important observation as it demonstrates how interactions with literacy, and indeed features of literacy skill, are changing in line with technological advances. The importance of touch within literacy activity is highlighted above in connection with reading, but other studies have shown that the same is true of writing. For example Price et al. (2015) observed children aged 2–3 years old as they engaged in a free finger painting activity and a colouring-in activity in both paper and digital environments (the digital environment used an iPad). While the study indicated that there were benefits and limitations to each environment, they discovered that the use of the iPad extended mark making by 'enabling continuous marking and dynamic changes in touch types' (p. 138). They concluded that the ability to make continuous stroke and circular movements suggests particular benefits for younger children learning to write as this provides a foundation for mark making with other tools (such as pen or pencil), as well as contributing to the development of more sophisticated digital literacy skills.

The research discussed above has shown how digital technology, and iPads in particular, have been seen to support children's literacy skills. However, by focusing on this from the perspective of the child we are forced to recognise that the very concept of 'literacy skill' is a changing and dynamic construct. This section has demonstrated that technology such as tablets can be highly motivating and engaging for young children; however, if we are to build on the affordances of this technology then it is vital that we recognise how constructions of literacy are changing. We have shown how *touch* is now fundamental to the ways in which young children learn to read and write, both independently and in collaboration with others, yet further research is required in order to understand how adults can support these aspects of literacy development in the classroom. This same issue has also been highlighted in relation to numeracy. The next section focuses on the learning of numeracy and explores the ways in which digital technology has facilitated children's mathematical thinking.

Technology and numeracy

Papert's (1980) Logo work offered an early and exciting vision of how digital technology might transform the teaching and learning of mathematics. Most of the research in mathematics education involving the use of digital technology has focused on the middle and high school levels – in part because of the way in which hardware and software design targeted older learners, and in part because the use of digital technologies in the early grades has traditionally encountered opposition by those concerned that children at this age need tactile, concrete experiences. Indeed, the early years (ages 5–7) mathematics classroom has long featured the use of physical manipulatives such as counters, Cuisinaire rods and 10-frames.

More recently, several researchers have argued for the appropriateness and benefit of using 'virtual manipulatives' (VMs) in the early years, which build on the familiarity of physical ones, but which may also provide a range of added affordances. These researchers call into question the assumption that 'concrete' tools are more appropriate for young children, and argue that physical manipulatives may actually limit children's mathematical expressivity. Sarama and Clements (2009) point specifically to the potential that virtual manipulatives (and other well-designed software) have for supporting the development of *integrated-concrete* knowledge, which interconnects knowledge of physical objects, actions on these objects and symbolic representations of these objects and actions. They outline seven affordances that existing research on young children's use of well-designed technology has found: (1) bringing mathematical ideas and action to conscious awareness; (2) encouraging and facilitating complete, precise explanations; (3) supporting mental 'actions on objects'; (4) changing the very nature of the manipulative; (5) symbolising mathematical concept; (6) linking the concrete and the symbolic with feedback; (7) and recording and replaying student actions.

In the specific area of numeracy, a wide range of digital technologies have been developed and studied, including desktop computer software, internet-based applets, touchscreen applications and, of course, calculators. Research suggests that children whose learning occurs in rich environments that include (virtual) manipulatives tend to learn better and reach higher levels of academic achievement (e.g. Steen et al., 2006). However, the presence of the manipulative is not sufficient: their effectiveness depends on how these manipulatives are designed and used (Goodwin and Highfield, 2013). For the most part, the benefits of virtual manipulatives are seen as augmenting those of physical ones by providing more precision (such as a calculation, a measurement or a geometric shape), more feedback that is mathematically relevant and by demanding more mathematical forms of expression (through numbers, symbols or actions). The feedback is very important since it allows children to learn from their actions, rather than relying on the evaluative feedback of a teacher. The mathematical expressivity is important because it enables children to inhabit a world in which communication and manipulation is done through mathematics – a kind of 'Mathland' as Papert (1980) called it.

A numeracy example of this is the base-ten blocks, which have been used as the basis for several virtual manipulatives such as internet-based applets. One specific affordance of the virtual base-ten blocks is the automatic transformation of a 10-block into 10 individual unit blocks when moved from a 10s column into a 1s column (see Base Blocks from the National Library of Virtual Manipulatives [NLVM]). This enables learners to see how the column location affects the meaning of the block while also enabling a particular action (moving the block from one column to another) to mediate the mathematical idea of place value. Although no empirical evidence for the effect of such a design choice has been reported, its presence in other virtual manipulatives, such as Kortenkamp's Place Value (an iPad app), indicates some consensus about its desirability. Another specific affordance is the way in which the virtual manipulatives show and update the numerical value of the tokens, blocks or chips placed in the different columns, thereby providing symbolic feedback and reducing the need for children to calculate. This affordance is very important in a mathematics learning context because it means that children who may not have certain number sense fluency can still engage in more advanced mathematical activity.

In addition to VMs, there have also been several software programs that have been developed for young children that are not directly based on physical manipulatives.

For example, Numberbonds (also developed for the iPad) has a tetris-like set-up in which a coloured rod falls in an area with a set length and the player has to quickly choose another rod (options are displayed on the screen) that together with the falling one will make a given length (such as 10 for example). This is a level-based game that has been studied by neuroscientists and cognitive psychologists, who have found positive effects (see Butterworth, 2011). Unlike the previous example, Numberbonds addresses only one small component of the activities enabled by physical manipulatives such as Cuisinaire rods. Also, in contrast with the previous example, in which children could manipulate mathematical objects, this game is more instructive in that it promotes procedural learning, relying on evaluative feedback and repetitive interactions with imposed representations. Research has found that although such instructive technologies can improve specific skills (Riconscente, 2013), they frequently do not provide opportunities for learners to manipulate or express new mathematical meanings. Indeed, in her study of children aged 5–8 years old, Goodwin (2009) found that using manipulable digital technologies resulted in the production of more 'developed and advanced representations' than those using an instructive digital technology (cited in Goodwin and Highfield, 2013: 208). Further, and of particular significance to our interest in this chapter, these researchers note that using instructive digital technology focused children more on receiving positive feedback than on discussing or reflecting on the embedded mathematical concept.

The examples in this section have been designed for the mouse and keyboard inputs available with desktop and laptop computers. The main interaction is through clicking (rather than typing) on discrete objects, with one child working with the software at a time. The recent arrival of tablet technology has enabled digital technology interactions to become more immediate, as the fingers contact the screen directly, either through tapping or a wide variety of gestures. Further, for applications that are multitouch, the screen can be touched by multiple fingers as well as multiple users at the same time. These new applications are all the more intriguing in light of emerging neuroscientific literature pointing to the importance of fingers in the development of number sense (e.g. Andres et al., 2007; Gracia-Bafalluy and Noël, 2008; Sato et al., 2007).

As with computer-based technologies, there exists a range of design choices. There are more instructive examples such as Fingu (Barendregt et al., 2012), an iPad application in which the stimuli are given as fixed arrangements of floating objects and children must place the corresponding number of fingers on the screen simultaneously. Each touch produces a fingerprint, after which evaluative feedback is given (auditory signal as well as visual cues). The game is timed and at each of the seven levels the number of objects that appear increases while the time to respond decreases. The necessity for simultaneous rather than sequential input further encourages *subitising*, which is an important component of number sense (and involves visually identifying, without counting, the number of objects in a given set). A study conducted with 5- and 6-year-olds indicates that after playing for a three-week period, with guidance from the teacher, the children increased their percentage of right answers (Barendregt et al., 2012).

In the next section of this chapter, we will discuss TouchCounts (Sinclair and Jackiw, 2014), which is also an iPad application that is much less instructive. Briefly, there are two worlds: enumerating and operating (Figure 6.1a). The former features an ordinal model of numbers and the latter a cardinal model of numbers. In the Enumerating World, each finger tap produces a yellow disc. Tapping the screen four times consecutively will produce four discs, each numbered 1, 2, 3, 4, respectively, and four sounds 'one', 'two', 'three', 'four'. The discs fall off the bottom of the screen unless gravity is turned off, in which case they remain on the screen, or unless the finger tap is made above the horizontal line, which acts as a 'shelf' on which the discs rest (Figure 6.1b) (video: http://tinyurl.com/q8lpzrc). In the Operating World, tapping the screen with four fingers simultaneously produces a 'herd' with the numeral 4 on it, as well as four smaller discs (see Figure 6.1c). Multiple herds can be combined by using a pinching gesture (4 and 1 are being combined in Figure 6.1c). The resulting herd will be labelled with the sum, and this sum is said aloud. A herd can be partitioned into two herds by using a splitting gesture (video: http://tinyurl.com/omancvf).

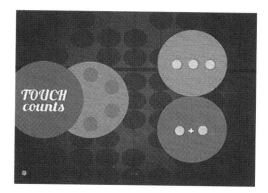

Figure 6.1a   Enumerating World (•••) and the Operating World (•+•)

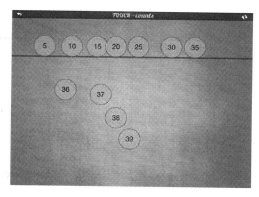

Figure 6.1b   Ordinal numbers falling off the shelf

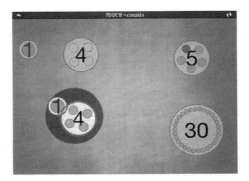

Figure 6.1c   Combining the numerals 4 and 1 in TouchCounts' Operating World

This type of interaction involves various number sense component abilities such as subitising and fine motor skills (e.g. simultaneous touch to generate the proper enumeration and dragging of a selected finger to place the circle on the line), but the environment may also help lay foundations for the counting principles and for the transition from ordinality to cardinality. This is because it can foster the development of awareness of the one-to-one correspondence between fingers and numerosities, or between numbers and successive touch-actions on the screen (one-to-one correspondence principle); it may foster memorisation of the sequence of number-words to recite when counting (stable order principle); in the modality without gravity, the last word heard through the audio feedback corresponds to the total number of circles on the screen (cardinality principle); and finally in the gravity mode the possibility of marking certain numbers by dragging them on the line may favour a process of objectifying the number, which is necessary for operating on numbers.

Pilot studies indicate that with the use of certain tasks, 5–6-year-old children can learn to shift from thinking of number in terms of the process of counting (in terms of ordinality) to thinking of them as reified objects (Sinclair and Heyd-Metzuyanim, 2014). Further, with even younger children (3–4 years old), pilot research has shown that the task of placing fingers all-at-once on the screen can help develop their 'gestural subitizing' (Sinclair and Pimm, 2015). Finally, the use of TouchCounts seems to encourage children's attention towards symbols, which in turn has been shown to support their ordinal understanding of numbers (Coles, 2014), which predicts future mathematical achievement (Lyons et al., 2014).

In general, while the affordances of tablet-based applications seem clearly geared to supporting young children's learning of number sense, more research is needed – not just on the use of the applications on their own, but also in concert with the more pervasive pencil-and-paper media of the mathematics classroom. One of the areas of research that has been underdeveloped relates to the social interactions that the use of digital technologies might occasion and how they might relate to emotional aspects of children's experiences, as well as to the development of literacy skills. In this chapter, we take the opportunity to delve into the relationship between numeracy and literacy in children's interactions with TouchCounts with the hope of better understanding the way in which more open-ended and non-instructive environments can support children's learning of *how to learn*. The next section presents some data on three 6-year-old children who were observed using TouchCounts. We draw from these data to show how the application not only supported the children's understanding of number but facilitated a whole variety of other skills including those pertaining to literacy.

CASE STUDY 1   'JUST 10'

We present the transcript of a short videoed episode involving three 6-year-old children (Naomi, Whyles and Auden – all pseudonyms) working with two researchers (including the second author) on the task of placing 'just 10' on the shelf. Naomi has the iPad in front of her and tries the task many times before finally succeeding. The two boys watch and comment as she makes successive attempts. The children are all in an after-school daycare.

The children had all successfully counted to 20 before work on the task began. As the literature shows, however, counting often begins as a memorised sequence of sounds, much like a song, in which children are not necessarily aware of the different numbers in the song, how those numbers are related to each other, or how counting can be used to determine the number of objects in a given set. Unfortunately, a child's ability to count to 20 is often taken as sufficient to move on to teaching addition. As we will highlight, children's understanding of number is much more complex. This becomes very evident when children use TouchCounts to count, because they have to relate the finger tapping, with the number naming, as well as the number symbol. Further, tasked with putting 'just 10' on the shelf, involves knowing how 10 relates to 7, 8 and 9. In particular, it involves knowing that 9 comes right before 10. This would be like knowing what word comes right before 'where' in the song *Twinkle, Twinkle, Little Star*.

After Naomi taps too many times on her first attempt, Nathalie shows her how to press the reset button so that she can start over. On her next attempt, Naomi puts the first tap above the shelf, which makes the others laugh and Naomi smile, indicating that it seems unlikely that Naomi is mistaking 1 for 10. Instead, this highlights the complexity of the task that Naomi has been given, which is not just to count, but to tap the screen in a very particular way. In other words, succeeding at the task involves a coordination of her hands on the screen, in addition to an awareness of the fact that the number immediately preceding 10 is 9. The complexity of getting 'just 10' on the shelf is evident in the fact that she tries three more times, without prompt (by pressing the reset button herself and starting over), putting 8 on the shelf first, and then 9, and then letting 10 fall away. On the fourth try, Naomi succeeds, with the help of Whyles, who points to the screen after she has reached 9.

In total, Naomi attempted the task eight times. Each time she taps on the screen, she sees numbered discs fall away or rest on the shelf, and she hears the number names. She seems to use this feedback to help her understand that she has not succeeded and decide to try again. Aside from the time she

(Continued)

(Continued)

puts 1 on the shelf right away, Naomi taps at least six times before hesitating. This suggests that she is more fluent with numbers up to 6, and knows that 10 will come after these numbers, but she is less sure about the order of the numbers between 7 and 10. Indeed, she puts 7 on the shelf once, 8 on the shelf twice, 9 on the shelf once and lets 10 fall away twice too. What can be seen in the video is that she slows down as she reaches past 6, which might suggest that she is attending either to the number symbols or the number names (or both) in an effort to figure out when she can expect 10 to arrive.

Encounters with TouchCounts

We would like to highlight two aspects of numeracy that arose in this activity: the developing awareness of ordinality and the subordination of counting to the task of putting 'just 10' on the shelf.

Developing awareness of ordinality

This task calls for Naomi to attend to the relation between numbers; that is the relation between 7 and 8 or between 9 and 10. This relation includes both order (8 is bigger than 7) and sequence (10 is bigger than 8 but is right after 9). This pertains to the ordinal aspect of number. The cardinal aspect of number links numbers to collections, for example the number '4' denotes a group of four objects. Recent research suggests that the current emphasis in primary school mathematics teaching of number on cardinal may be misplaced (Coles, 2014). Alternative curriculum approaches found in Gattegno (1974) posit that an awareness of number arises out of linguistic skill in a manner that does not emphasise a cardinal focus on counting collections. Linguistic skill and awareness of relations (which are aspects of ordinality) can be used to answer questions such as 'What number is one bigger than a million?' In addition, recent research in neuroscience shows how a significant aspect of the meaning of a numeral, for students who are successful at mathematics, is relational and strongly tied to the unfolding of the sequence of numerals (Lyons and Beilock, 2011). This research shows that beginning at age 2, a child's ability to assess the relative order of number symbols is an increasingly strong predictor of mathematical achievement.

We contend that as she tries to get 10 on the shelf, Naomi is not focused on 10 as a cardinal number, that is, on 10 as a label for the quantity of discs on the screen. Instead, she is developing an awareness of ordinality in that her interactions with TouchCounts involve a linguistic and symbolic attention to the relation between numbers – attention that is enabled by the fact that the application speaks the numbers and displays the symbols. Naomi watches and listens many times before she starts to focus on what precedes 10. What TouchCounts offers that many other manipulatives for early number learning do not, is the simultaneous correspondence between the aural number name, the number symbol and the finger tapping.

Physical manipulatives do not usually announce their number or display their number symbol. Further, Naomi controls the creation of the numbers, and thus the saying of the numbers and appearance of the symbols. This means that she can pause and listen to, or look at what she had made, which enables her to attend to the relation between the sounds ('eight' and 'nine') as well as the relation between the symbols (8 and 9).

Feedback and self-assessment

In relation to the point above, the fact that the numbers announce and display themselves means that Naomi receives significant feedback from TouchCounts. She does not need the teacher, or the other students, to tell her that she has made an error when she puts 8 on the shelf. Not only does she receive this direct feedback, in a non-evaluative manner, but it is feedback that can help her succeed. At the very least, she may infer that she needs to see/hear eight before she taps above the shelf (although she may think that 8 will be followed by 10!). The quick uptake of the reset button and the immediacy with which Naomi tries again, each time suggests that she is engaged in a number exploration that she wants to succeed at, and that she does not depend on the external evaluation of the teacher (or other classmate).

Collaborative interaction and literacy learning

Although TouchCounts is a maths application and has been designed to promote engagement with mathematical concepts, the data clearly indicated that the application provided an opportunity for collaborative learning that involved a use of many skills including those pertaining to numeracy and literacy. The data revealed a great deal of engagement from all three children, despite the fact that Naomi was the only child actually physically interacting with the iPad. For example, Whyles sat close to Naomi throughout the activity and his gaze was focused largely on the screen. As Naomi touched the screen, you could see his fingers twitching with each touch. Each time that Naomi failed to 'make 10' he rocked backwards and threw his hands over his mouth, showing that he was deeply engrossed in the process of reaching 10, even though he was not actually touching the iPad himself. As Naomi got nearer to achieving the goal, Whyles got closer to the screen. After a number of attempts, Naomi almost managed to reach the required number but did not realise that she needed to touch above 'the shelf' in order to complete the game. At this point Whyles simply pointed to the 'shelf' and Naomi was able to 'make 10'.

Like Whyles, the data indicated that Auden was also deeply engaged with the game. He rocked backwards and forwards in excitement and his gaze rested on the screen while Naomi was touching the iPad. At first Auden thought that the aim of the game was to 'make 5' rather than 10 so he called out 'Oh she missed, um, 5' during an early attempt, and then said 'Ugh, you missed it' when Naomi went beyond 5 in a later attempt. This shows that Auden understood the principle of the game and was engaged with the activity, even though he had initially misunderstood what the target number was.

Throughout this activity the children were all learning about a numerical concept; however, the activity also seemed to promote sophisticated levels of social interaction. Throughout the activity the boys made no attempt to touch the iPad or prevent Naomi from achieving the goal for herself, even though they were clearly very excited and engaged with the game. In addition, they each spontaneously offered Naomi some appropriate 'help' which was given through verbal and non-verbal means. This episode reflects the work of Flewitt et al. (2015), who also identified that iPads offered innovative opportunities for young children's literacy learning, both as independent learners but also as collaborative learners who needed to communicate effectively.

As discussed in the opening sections of this chapter, young children have been seen to interact with technology in ways that are almost innate (Prensky, 2001a). In particular, research has indicated that children's motivation to succeed in iPad activities has 'sometimes led them to display more advanced literacy skills than staff had previously given them credit for' (Flewitt et al., 2015: 299). Yet further study has concluded that as research into the ways in which children learn through their interactions with digital media is still relatively new, we do not yet fully understand how children's literacy learning, and indeed any other learning, can be scaffolded by adults (Wolfe and Flewitt, 2010).

The episode discussed in this section provides some insight into this. As described above, as Naomi touches the iPad, the application produces a voice that counts out the numbers. During an early attempt at the game Naomi accidently brushes a few of her knuckles onto the screen when touching the screen to 'make 10'. As a result the iPad voice says 'One, Two, Three, Seven'. All three of the children are clearly confused by this and they all immediately look to the researcher for guidance. The researcher takes Naomi's hand and points to her other fingers saying, 'you know what happens – if you touch with a lot of your parts of your fingers'. Naomi smiles briefly in acknowledgement and responds 'Oh' before resetting the game and starting again. The other two children look to the screen, indicating that they too have understood and are ready to watch Naomi start again. Careful analysis of the data, taken from the perspective of the child, illuminates the importance of the adult in supporting the children's learning within the context of the technology. It was important that the adult explained why the iPad had jumped from '3' to '7', otherwise the immediate learning experience would have been curtailed. The children may also have begun to lose interest in the game as well as the motivation or confidence to come back to it.

It is also noteworthy that the game facilitated an opportunity for the adult to explain something about touch technology that was not only crucial for this game, but has implications for many other interactions with digital technology. As mentioned earlier, Simpson et al.'s study (2013) highlighted how interactions with literacy, and features of literacy skill, are changing in line with technological advances due to the role of touch. They argued that touch was directly linked to cognitive awareness, as each touch needed to be 'employed at a specific velocity and appropriate level of pressure' (p. 129) if the tablet was to respond as intended. This suggests that while the children using the TouchCounts application were learning about an important mathematical concept, the adult was also scaffolding their learning in relation to the technology, which in turn would have supported all future interactions with touch-based technology.

SUMMARY

This chapter has shown how digital technology is providing young children with opportunities to promote their development in numeracy and literacy. We have demonstrated that exploratory, touchscreen technology can encourage children to interact with text in ways that have not previously been possible. Technology can afford children opportunities to not only gain knowledge and practise skills, but also engage with concepts in a way that promotes confidence and motivation for learning. This was evidenced in the case study presented above, where three 6-year-old children were observed using TouchCounts. The data revealed that while the application provided an opportunity for children to learn and develop important mathematical constructs, there was also a great deal of collaborative learning taking place which included skills and knowledge associated with literacy and numeracy. For example, it was apparent that this application focused children's attention on sign and symbol systems, which are crucial to development in literacy and numeracy as well as *learning* in general. Moreover the data revealed that as the feedback given to children from TouchCounts was helpful and non-evaluative, this encouraged children to maintain motivation and engagement with the activity. This engagement was observed in all of the children involved in the activity, including those who were not directly interacting with the iPad.

While this chapter has highlighted the importance of technology in children's learning of numeracy and literacy, one particular feature that has been emphasised is the role of touchscreen technology. As discussed, literature has shown that touch is now embedded in the ways in which children read, write and develop number sense. What is more, touch is not just a physical function but is part of a cognitive process through which children make sense of texts and *learn*. Multitouch offers even more opportunities for engagement as many fingers, hands and children can be manipulating at once. As the TouchCounts example highlighted, adults have a role to play in supporting children's interactions with touch technology; however, if we are to capitalise on the affordances of technology such as iPads, we need to understand more about the ways in which children utilise touch. This signals a clear need for further research into the ways in which young children interact with technology and use multitouch to engage with screen texts. Only then will we be able to build on the affordances of technology, and not only support young children in their development of numeracy and literacy, but help them to become confident and motivated *learners*.

References and further reading

Alliance for Childhood (2004) *Tech Tonic: Towards a New Literacy of Technology*. College Park, MD: Alliance for Childhood.

Andres, M., Seron, X. and Oliver, E. (2007) Contribution of hand motor circuits to counting. *Journal of Cognitive Neuroscience* 19(4): 563–576.

Barendregt, W., Lindstrom, B., Rietz-Leppanen, E., et al. (2012) Development and evaluation of Fingu: A mathematics iPad game using multi-touch interaction. Paper presented at Interaction, Design and Children 2012, 12–15 June, Bremen, Germany, pp. 1–4.

Bearne, E., Clark, C., Johnson, A., et al. (2007) *Reading on Screen*. Leicester: United Kingdom Literacy Association.

Berson, I.R. and Berson M.J. (eds) (2010) *High Tech Tots: Childhood in a Digital World*. Charlotte, NC: Information Age Publishing.

Buckingham D. (2000) *After the Death of Childhood: Growing Up in the Age of Electronic Media*. Oxford: Polity Press.

Butterworth, B. (2011) Dyscalculia: From brain to education. *Science* 332(6033): 1049–1053.

Carrington, V. and Robinson, M. (eds) (2009) *Digital Literacies: Social Learning and Classroom Practices*. London: Sage.

Coles, A. (2014) Ordinality, neuro-science and the early learning of number. In C. Nichol, S. Oesterle, P. Liljedahl and D. Allen (eds), *Proceedings of the Joint PME 38 and PME-NA 36 Conference*, Vol. 2. Vancouver, BC: Psychology of Mathematics Education, pp. 329–336.

Duncan, G.J., Dowsett, C.J., Claessens, A., et al. (2007) School readiness and later achievement. *Developmental Psychology* 43(6): 1428–1446.

Flewitt, R., Messer, D. and Kucirkova, N. (2015) New directions for early literacy in a digital age: The iPad, *Journal of Early Childhood Literacy* 15(3): 289–310.

Gattegno, C. (1974) *The Common Sense of Teaching Mathematics*. New York: Education Solution Worldwide Inc. Retrieved from: www.calebgattegno.org/teaching-mathematics.html (accessed December 2016).

Goodwin, K. (2009) *Impact and affordances of interactive multimedia*. Unpublished PhD Thesis. Macquarie University, Sydney.

Goodwin, K. and Highfield, K. (2013) A framework for examining technologies and early mathematics learning. In L.D. English and J.T. Mulligan (eds), *Reconceptualising Early Mathematics Learning*. New York: Springer, pp. 205–226.

Gracia-Bafalluy, M. and Noël, M. (2008) Does finger training increase young children's numerical performance? *Cortex* 44(4): 368–375.

Hsin, C.-T., Li, M.-C. and Tsai, C.-C. (2014) The influence of young children's use of technology on their learning: A review. *Educational Technology and Society* 17(4): 85–99.

LeFevre, J., Skwarchuk, S., Smith-Chant, B., Fast, L., Kamawar., D. and Bisanz, J. (2009) Home numeracy experiences and children's math performance in the early school years, *Canadian Journal of Behavioural Science* 41(2): 55–66.

Levy, R. (2008) 'Third spaces' are interesting places: Applying 'third space theory' to nursery-aged children's constructions of themselves as readers. *Journal of Early Childhood Literacy* 8(1): 43–66.

Levy, R. (2009) 'You have to understand words ... but not read them': Young children becoming readers in a digital age. *Journal of Research in Reading* 32(1): 75–91.

Levy, R. (2011) Young children, digital technology and interaction with text. In M. Thomas (ed.), *Deconstructing Digital Natives*. London: Routledge pp. 151–168.

Levy, R. and Thompson, P. (2015) Creating 'buddy partnerships' with 5- and 11-year-old boys: A methodological approach to conducting participatory research with young children. *Journal of Early Childhood Research* 13(2): 137–149.

Lukie, I.K., Skwarchuk, S., Lefevre, J. and Sowinski, C. (2014) The role of child interests and collaborative parent–child interactions in fostering numeracy and literacy development in Canadian homes. *Early Childhood Education Journal* 42(4): 251–259.

Lyons, I. and Beilock, S. (2011) Numerical ordering ability mediates the relation between number-sense and arithmetic competence. *Cognition* 121(2): 256–261.

Lyons I., Price G., Vaessen A., Blomert L. and Ansari D. (2014) Numerical predictors of arithmetic success in grades 1–6. *Developmental Science* 17(5): 714–726.

Manolitsis, G., Georgiou, G.K. and Tziraki, N. (2013) Examining the effects of home literacy and numeracy environment on early reading and math acquisition. *Early Childhood Research Quarterly* 28(4): 692–703.

Marsh, J. and Singleton, C. (2009) Editorial: Literacy and technology: Questions of reading. *Journal of Research in Reading* 32(1): 1–5.

Marsh, J., Brookes, G., Hughes, J., et al. (2005) *Digital Beginnings: Young Children's Use of Popular Culture, Media and New Technologies*. Sheffield: Literacy Research Centre, University of Sheffield.

Marsh, J., Plowman, L., Yamada-Rice, et al. (2015) *Exploring Play and Creativity in Pre-Schoolers' Use of Apps: Final Project Report*. Retrieved from: www.techandplay.org (accessed 27 January 2017).

Merchant, G. (2007) Writing in the future in the digital age. *Literacy* 41(3): 118–128.

Miller, E.B. and Warschauer, M. (2014) Young children and e-reading: Research to date and questions for the future. *Learning, Media and Technology* 39(3): 283–305.

Moll, L.C., Amanti, C., Neff, D. and Gonzalez, N. (1992) Funds of knowledge for teaching: Using a qualitative approach to connect homes and classrooms. *Theory into Practice* 31(2): 132–141.

Papert, S. (1980) *Mindstorms: Children, Computers and Powerful Ideas*. New York: Basic Books.

Plowman, L., McPake, J. and Stephen, C. (2010) The technologisation of childhood? Young children and technology in the home. *Children and Society* 24(1): 63–74.

Plowman, L., Stevenson, O., Stephen, C. and McPake, J. (2012) Preschool children's learning with technology at home. *Computers and Education* 59(1): 30–37.

Prensky, M. (2001) Digital natives, digital immigrants part 1. *On the Horizon* 9(5): 1–6.

Price, S., Jewitt, C. and Crescenzi, L. (2015) The role of iPads in pre-school children's mark making development. *Computers and Education* 87: 131–141.

Purpura, D.J., Hume, L.E., Sims, D.M. and Lonigan, C.J. (2011) Early literacy and early numeracy: The value of including early literacy skills in the prediction of numeracy development. *Journal of Experimental Child Psychology* 110(4): 647–658.

Riconscente, M. (2013) *Mobile Learning Game Improves 5th Graders' Fractions Knowledge and Attitudes*. Los Angeles, CA: GameDesk Institute. Retrieved from: www.gamedesk.org/projects/motion-math-in-class (accessed 27 January 2017).

Sarama, J. and Clements, D.H. (2009) 'Concrete' computer manipulatives in mathematics education. *Child Development Perspectives* 3(3): 145–150.

Sato, M., Cattaneo, L., Rizzolatti, G. and Gallese, V. (2007) Numbers within our hands: Modulation of corticospinal excitability of hand muscles during numerical judgment. *Journal of Cognitive Neuroscience* 19(4): 684–693.

Scott, J. (2000) Children as respondents. In P. Christensen and A. James (eds), *Research with Children: Perspectives and Practices*. London: Routledge pp. 98–119.

Simpson, A., Walsh, M. and Rowsell, J. (2013) The digital reading path: Researching modes and multidirectionality with iPads. *Literacy* 47(3): 123–130.

Sinclair, N. and Heyd-Metzuyanim, E. (2014) Learning number with *TouchCounts*: The role of emotions and the body in mathematical communication. *Technology, Knowledge and Learning* 19(1): 81–99.

Sinclair, N. and Jackiw, N. (2014) TouchCounts [software application for the iPad].

Sinclair, N. and Pimm, D. (2015) Whatever be their number: Counting on the visible, the audible, and the tangible. In M. Meletiou-Mavrotheris, K. Mavrou and E. Paparistodemou (eds), *Integrating Touch-Enabled and Mobile Devices into Contemporary Mathematics Education*. Hershey, PA: IGI Global, pp. 50–80.

Steen, K., Brookes, D. and Lyon, T. (2006) The impact of virtual manipulatives on first grade geometry instruction and learning. *Journal of Computers in Mathematics and Science Teaching* 25(4): 373–391.

Weber, D. (2006) Media use by infants and toddlers: A potential for play. In D. Singer, R. Golinkoff and K. Hirsh-Pasek (eds), *Play=Learning: How Play Motivates and Enhances Children's Cognitive and Socio-Emotional Growth*. New York: Oxford University Press, pp. 169–191.

Wolfe, S. and Flewitt, R. (2010) New technologies, new multimodal literacy practices and young children's metacognitive development. *Cambridge Journal of Education* 40(4): 387–399.

7

UNDER 3s AND TECHNOLOGY

Jane O'Connor

CHAPTER OVERVIEW

Throughout the other chapters in this book, references are continually made to the abundance of debate and research about children and technologies. Yet very little research is currently available about children under 3 years old using technologies, despite the fact that children are using internet-enabled resources at this young age (Marsh et al., 2016; Palaiologou, 2016). This chapter begins to offer some initial insights into this area, and will cover:

- An overview of existing research into very young children using touchscreen technology.
- The debate around whether very young children using touchscreens is detrimental or beneficial to their development, play and learning.
- A discussion of findings of an online parental survey exploring 0–3s' play with touchscreens in the UK and differing parental practices and attitudes towards this usage.
- Reflection on findings in terms of supporting parenting practice and further research.

Recent years have seen an enormous rise in the ownership and use of touchscreen technology such as tablets, smartphones and other mobile devices in many homes in the UK (Ofcom, 2014). These devices potentially offer the very youngest children (from around 6 months of age) the opportunity to engage with the digital world as interfaces on touchscreen devices are immediately accessible using swipes and drags with fingers. The extent to which touchscreen technology is incorporated into the lives of very young children, and indeed whether it should be incorporated at all, is becoming increasingly recognised as a modern-day parenting dilemma (Cocozza, 2014). This chapter looks at the findings of an online survey of UK parents about their 0–3 year olds' play with touchscreens and their reflections on the potential benefits and disadvantages of such usage, particularly in relation to traditional definitions of play and learning. The chapter will conclude by reflecting on the implications of the rising use of touchscreens by 0–3s for parents and carers. First, though, the chapter reviews the key developmental milestones of children in this age group and reflects on the design features of touchscreens which enable and encourage such young children to engage with this technology.

0–3s developmental play, learning and touchscreen technology

Apart from in utero, the 0–3 age range encompasses the most extreme period of development for children in their lifetime (Berk, 2012). What follows is a simplified summary of a complex area in order to outline the key developmental milestones that most children are expected to reach by age 6 months, 1 year, 18 months, 2 years and 3 years, along with an indication of how children of these ages might typically be able to interact with touchscreens (Table 7.1). The information is taken from the *Milestone Moments* published by the United States Centers for Disease Control (CDC) and from Hourcade et al.'s (2015) analysis of YouTube videos of infants and toddlers using tablets.

Prior to the wide availability of tablets and touchscreens, children of up to 3 or 4 years of age were restricted in their interaction with technology by the interfaces of keyboard and mouse. As Hourcade et al. (2015: 19) note, 'Touchscreens have lifted this restriction, as interacting through touch matches the motor abilities of much younger children.' In his study of iPads, story apps and early literacy, Merchant (2015: 11) also notes specific features of touchscreens that particularly appeal to young children such as their 'weight, portability and intuitive touchscreen interface'. Furthermore, given the way in which children are highly motivated to use the real tools and technology that are normally reserved for older children or adults (Wohlwend, 2009) it is unsurprising that even very young children are often excited and keen to start playing with, and exploring, the tablets and touchscreens that many of them live with in their home environment. Clearly, touchscreens have provided the very youngest of children with new developmentally achievable opportunities for engaging with technology which require careful scrutiny and investigation in order to ensure such practices are of benefit to the developing child.

The following section details current research around 0–3s' play with touchscreens in order to situate the issue within ongoing debates over what is considered appropriate in relation to very young children's use of technology in the home environment. It is important to acknowledge here that much research is being conducted in relation to the use of touchscreen technology in nurseries and other preschool settings with children aged 3 or 4 years old (for example, see Verenikina and Kervin, 2012). While some issues are clearly common to both areas, the focus of this chapter is on the use of such technology in the home as this is the environment all children experience from birth and where the perceptions and attitudes of their parents/carers have maximum impact on their opportunity to engage with touchscreen technology. The use of technology by children under 3 in the home environment is also an under-researched area that is often overlooked in larger studies.

Table 7.1 Developmental milestones and potential touchscreen use.

Age	Developmental milestones	Interaction with touchscreens
Up to 6 months	Usually: Able to recognise familiar faces, play with others and respond to emotions. Can recognise their name, respond to sounds by making sounds and are curious about items around them, often reaching for them or bringing them to their mouth. Begin to sit without support.	Typically: Attracted by the sounds and images of touchscreens. May interact with them with their flattened hands or mouths.
By 1 year	Respond to simple spoken requests, use simple gestures and are beginning to use simple words. Explore objects by interacting with them in various physical ways, look at the right picture/object when it is named, copy gestures and can poke with the index finger.	Simple interactions with a touchscreen device such as opening an app by touching it or swiping through photos stored on the device. In their study Hourcade et al. (2015) found that a majority of children between 12 and 17 months can understand and use basic apps.
18 months	Most children can: Walk alone, drink from a cup and eat with a spoon, speak several words, hand objects to others as part of play, show affection to loved ones and use pointing gestures to bring attention to something, participate in pretend play and are able to scribble.	The use of purposeful pointing and scribbling suggests more advanced interactions with touchscreens is possible, such as playing simple touch games and using drawing apps.
2 years	Frequently copy behaviour they see in parents and older children and typically enjoy playing with other children. Recognise the names of familiar people and objects, follow simple instructions. Speak using short sentences and repeat words. May be able to sort items by shape and colour, play make-believe games, show hand preference and name items in a picture book. Can often make copies of straight lines and circles.	Touchscreen use could be more sophisticated at this age when playing games, drawing and manipulating apps. The Hourcade et al. (2015) study found that 90% of children at this age displayed at least moderate ability to use touchscreens.
3 years	Typically show a wide range of emotions, show empathy for others and can take turns in a game. Can follow instructions with two or three steps and can name most familiar things. Can work toys with buttons, levers and moving parts, do simple jigsaw puzzles and build blocks into a tower. Can climb, run and ride a tricycle.	May be able to use touchscreens to create pictures, follow stories, play more complex games involving matching words/sounds and images and enjoy socialising with family/friends via Skype.

As Kucirkova et al. (2013: 115) note: 'Very few studies, if any, have focused on children's engagement with iPads in situations in which children are most likely to encounter them, namely, in their homes.' Therefore there is value in drawing together here the existing research in the area, along with findings from a recent online parental survey in order to highlight key issues and dilemmas which this practice engenders.

Very young children's use of touchscreens: Current debates and research

Rates of ownership of touchscreens, and the usage of such devices by very young children, continue to rise. An Ofcom report in 2014 found that the number of households in England having tablet computers more than tripled from 20% in 2012 to 71% in 2014. The report claims 40% of 3–4 year olds use a tablet computer at home and 20% of children this age use a tablet computer to go online (no specific data are available in this report for children under 3). In relation to younger children, a US study (Common Sense Media, 2013) found 38% of children under 2 regularly use touchscreens (up from 10% in 2011). Furthermore, in her study of families in four European Countries, including England, Palaiologou (2016) found that the rate of children under 3 having access to digital technology, including tablets, was around 60%. As parents are the main gatekeepers of their young children's use of technology, it follows that their beliefs and behaviour in relation to parenting, child development and learning are instrumental in the access their 0–3s have to this technology.

Indeed, Flewitt (2012) found that parental beliefs have a significant impact on if and how children use digital media in the home environment, with the most positive attitudes reflecting higher rates of usage. In their study of preschoolers using technology in the home, Marsh et al. (2005) found that most parents encouraged and supported their children's early experiences with digital technologies because they believed that they would play a significant role in their children's education and future careers. The social nature of children learning through technology was also reinforced in this study as they found that many young children develop dispositions and competences with and through digital technology in the context of social interaction with their families and peers.

However, not all research findings have been so positive. Indeed, within the public and academic debate around young children and technology two key discourses are discernible – one in favour of children's use of technology and one completely against – along with many studies which represent a more considered view of the potential pros and cons of 0–3s using technology. The first discourse can be identified as emanating from a perception of children, particularly very young children, as innocent, natural and in need of shielding from the adult world (see Higonnet, 1998). Identifying with this position leads to protectionist behaviour around children and technology, whereby technology is seen as somehow robbing children of their childhoods. Palmer (2007) takes this stance when she writes about children today being polluted by (among other things) technology. This leads to them experiencing what she terms rather unpleasantly as 'toxic' childhoods. This type of panic mongering around technology is often picked up in the right wing press (for example, see Adams, 2014), further establishing the correlation between being a 'good parent' and protecting or limiting your child/ren's access to and use of technology. The rise of outdoor play movements such as 'Project Wild Thing' (Bond, 2013) and the identification of 'nature-deficit disorder' (Louv, 2010) can also be conceptualised as being less extreme manifestations of this discourse around childhood being more suitably aligned with the outdoor, social pursuits of nature rather than the indoor, often solitary, pursuits of technology (See Chapter 5 for more on outdoor play with technologies).

KEY DEFINITION

Nature-deficit disorder

The term 'nature-deficit disorder' was coined by Richard Louv in his book *Last Child in the Woods* (2010). It refers to how our societal disconnect with nature, and our plugged-in culture in the Western world, is affecting today's children by restricting outdoor play. Louv explains how some children are able to adapt to the overstimulation of modern society, but others can develop symptoms such as attention problems, obesity, anxiety and depression. Nature-deficit disorder is not a medical condition, rather it is a description of the human costs of alienation from nature.

In support of the protectionist discourse around children and technology there is also an emerging body of paediatric health research that suggests that minimising very young children's screen time in general may be beneficial to their wellbeing and development. For example, Radesky et al. (2014) explored whether media use was associated with self-regulation difficulties and found that 'infants and toddlers with self-regulation difficulties (i.e. problems with self-soothing, sleep, emotional regulation, and attention) view more media at two years of age, independent of other important confounders' (2014: 1173). In a further review of research specifically around mobile and interactive media use by young children, Radesky et al. (2015) note that there is little evidence that 30-month-old children derive any learning benefit from engaging with mobile media and are dependent on 'real-life' interactions for their cognitive and social development.

The alternative and, in many ways, opposing discourse is grounded in the growing recognition of the opportunities technology offers young children in terms of learning, playing and socialising. Also aligned to the concept of the 'good parent' is the belief that encouraging your children to use technology and enabling them to do so leads to better educational outcomes for them and, in time, a more successful experience in the world of work. This was demonstrated by Vittrup et al. (2016: 43), who explored parental perceptions in the USA of the role of media and technology in their young children's lives (2–7 year olds) and found that: 'Overall parents showed positive attitudes toward media, to the extent that they believed media exposure to be vital to children's development and many disagreed with recommendations from expert sources regarding age appropriate screen time.' They reported that 68.5% of the 101 parents surveyed agreed that 'introducing technological tools at a young age prepared children better for tomorrow's work force' and 33% of them believed that 'children may fall behind academically if their use of technological tools is restricted in early childhood' (Vittrup et al., 2016: 49). There have also been a limited number of small-scale case studies which have explored how touchscreens may help very young children to develop literacy skills. For example Kucirkova et al. (2013) used multimodal analysis to gain insights into the patterns of interaction which emerged when a mother and her 33-month-old daughter shared a self-created, audio-visual 'iPad story' app. They found that the use of such apps enriched the storytelling experience, suggesting that such new technologies may have an important role to play in supporting parent–child personalised stories.

Potential positive influences on the cognitive, brain and social development of children under 3 using touchscreens are currently being investigated by a team of researchers at the University of London. Professor Karmiloff-Smith, who is co-investigator on the project, explains how such a study is important because many parents are concerned about how using touchscreen devices may be affecting young children. She notes that: 'It is possible that babies might sometimes learn faster from tablets, with their moving pictures and sounds, than from static books. Studying how babies develop and learn is very important to their later education. We want to find out whether interactive use of tablets might indeed improve fine motor control, hand/eye co-ordination and visual attention' (Karmiloff-Smith, 2015).

The research evidence is clearly incomplete, emerging and somewhat contradictory as to whether allowing babies and toddlers to use touchscreens and mobile devices is an appropriate practice. This diversity of opinion is reflected in the following section, where the experiences and opinions held by a group of 226 parents of children under 3 in the UK who responded to an online survey about their children's use of touchscreen technology is discussed (O'Connor and Fotakopoulou, 2016). It is important to note that the respondents to the survey were largely middle-class professionals in their 30s and so were not representative of the diverse range of families across the UK. Therefore, the findings from the survey are intended to serve as an initial exploration of the current technological practices of babies and young children in the UK in relation to touchscreens, and as a way of including parental views on the subject in the ongoing debate.

Parents' stories

Where and in what ways do 0–3 year olds use touchscreen technology?

Responses to the survey indicated that the rate of children under 3 in middle-class homes in the UK using a smartphone, iPad or other tablet daily or sometimes, is 66%. Playing game apps was reported as the most popular use of touchscreens, identified by 92% of parents, with using learning/educational apps as the second most common usage at 67%. Looking at photos and watching video sources were also recorded as common uses of touchscreens. Thirty-seven per cent of parents reported their children used Skype or similar, while 24% said their 0–3s engaged with books on their touchscreens. As well as being used at home, parents also mentioned using touchscreens when on aeroplanes with their 0–3s and also at medical appointments and in waiting rooms to keep the child calm and occupied.

What do parents perceive as the benefits of their 0–3 year olds using touchscreens?

The use of touchscreens for learning new skills was the highest scoring benefit perceived by parents (72%), followed by using touchscreens for entertainment purposes (50%). Many responses focused on the ways in which parents felt that an early investment in learning how to use technology would be beneficial to their children at some point in the future. For example:

> It will help him adapt to the computer age.

> We live in a technological world, it's going to be an important skill in his lifetime.

Being a 'good parent' seems to be interpreted here as ensuring that their children are 'keeping up' with technological, and therefore social changes. Many parents talked candidly about using touchscreens for more practical reasons such as for distracting or controlling their very young children, for example:

> It can be an instant pleaser in places such as the car (my 2 year old hates car journeys) and occasionally if out eating, etc. and she is bored of drawing/playing it keeps her still.

> We use specific apps to help distract during medical procedures for child.

This recognition of very young children's fascination with touchscreens was also evident in parents' reporting of the way in which touchscreens were perceived to enable very young children to express their creativity, pursue knowledge or explore their own interests. Comments on this theme included the following:

> It's fun for them, and they see us doing it, but mainly it gives him access to a world of possibilities, mostly pictures, which is why I love the internet too.

> She can be very impatient when she cannot achieve something. Using the iPad has allowed her to learn to do something e.g. complete a puzzle before she was dexterous enough to complete a real one.

Another interesting category of responses focused on the opportunities touch-screens presented to very young children for communicating and connecting with absent family members, even over very long distances:

> We live a 3-hour drive from family and so being able to FaceTime with them on a regular basis is really important for us all. My daughter loves to see her family on FaceTime and I think it's important.

> Allows him to see and 'chat' with grandparents who live far away.

In a time of increasingly geographically disparate extended families due to changes in social mobility, employment patterns and globalisation it is clear that mobile touchscreen devices offer important opportunities for even very young children to develop relationships with distant family (see Kelly, 2013).

This use of touchscreens seemed to be uncontentious for the respondents and no negative comments were made about the facility for babies and toddlers to see and connect with physically absent friends and family.

What concerns do parents have about their 0–3 year olds using touchscreens?

The majority of parents (61.5%) reported having concerns about their 0–3s using touchscreens. Responses drew largely on the discourse of childhood innocence whereby children are perceived as primarily vulnerable, in need of guidance and protection with the adult knowing best and being the advocate for the child's wellbeing. A small number of respondents reported having no concerns at all about their under 3s using touchscreens and rationalised their use as no different from other activities such as reading books:

> No concerns as we limit access and use apps that restricts little ones' access to the rest of the phone.

> No, I don't understand why it is any different from a book, it's only bad if used inappropriately same as any other form of media, everything in balance.

Whereas others were so worried about negative effects that they allowed no use at all:

> We have not encouraged our daughter to use a touchscreen. We haven't even let her know it's possible to play games on devices, etc. It doesn't seem right to me that she might be potentially able to use a device very competently before she is able to speak properly.

> I would not let my son use anything other than the camera at this age [21 months]. He does not use the smartphone for anything else.

However, the majority of respondents (66%) allowed their under 3s to use touchscreens but 85% of them put limitations on their use (usually reported as 20–30 minutes per day). The range of concerns expressed about the practice fell into the following broad categories and seemed often to be compounded by lack of trusted official guidance and research-based evidence.

Becoming addicted/dependent

Many parents expressed fears that their child may become over-reliant or even addicted to their mobile devices. The following comments illustrate the unease many parents feel at allowing their children to use touchscreens and go some way to explaining their need for official guidelines on what limits they should be setting around their children's usage of the devices:

> I worry that he expects to play on it a lot and gets upset if I say no.

> Screens seem to be addictive in a way that books/toys are not.

Connected to these addiction concerns were worries about potential unknown unpleasant physical consequences of touchscreen use, which again aligned with the protectionist discourse around early childhood.

Worries about negative physical effects and developmental delay

Ensuring their very young children were learning to interact and communicate effectively was extremely important to the respondents. Examples of comments around this issue are provided below and represent significant first-hand observations of how touchscreen use may be interfering with this important area of development:

> In the very young babies if the screen is very close to their face ... it reduces the time they can spend looking at real people's faces and learning social skills.

> I believe it discourages social interaction. Also when people use them to occupy a child in a restaurant, for example, it is not teaching children how to interact in different social settings and in my opinion replaces one bad behaviour with a quieter one.

Parental fears also related to ways in which touchscreen use may impact negatively on their child's cognitive, social and physical development (including eyesight).

Touchscreen use replacing traditional play and learning

That very young children learn through play has become accepted in most of the developed world and forms the basis of many curricula and frameworks of early education, as well as informing health and education campaigns aimed at parents (see Patte and Brown, 2012). The strength of this discourse is reflected in the type of concerns the parents in this study have about touchscreens taking these learning opportunities away from their children by replacing traditional forms of play and print books.

> They very quickly start to want to play only on the iPad rather than anything else. The iPad version of reality is more colourful, easier and more appealing than real life (e.g. colouring in an iPad is much easier than on real paper with real pens). For this reason, we limit their use and do not allow access every day.

If they are on a tablet it's likely they will be watching video or playing games and this means they will not be doing other necessary activities like free, creative play, reading and exercise.

It seems clear from the type of concerns here and the lack of guidance on the issue that parental concerns around under 3s using touchscreens is an area which needs further research. Indeed, in this survey 95% of parents had had no guidance or information relating to their 0–3s using touchscreens from any source. Of the few parents who had had some advice this had been sourced by themselves from paediatric websites or from professional friends and colleagues. The lack of informed guidance, particularly around 'safe' lengths of time for 0–3s to use touchscreens, was a cause of concern for many parents.

Reflections on the findings of the survey

The responses to the survey revealed some important issues with implications for parenting practice and further research in the area. In relation to the enduring strength of established early childhood discourses around innocence and naturalness, the findings suggest that these continue to be instrumental in shaping the perceptions and beliefs of many parents of very young children. This is reflected in the concerns respondents expressed in relation to touchscreens potentially replacing traditional play and learning and fears around children accessing inappropriate material online. The issue of touchscreens replacing traditional play and learning is related to this as accepted middle-class constructions of being a 'good parent' have very much focused on encouraging children to read/be read print books and express themselves through physically creative and/or outdoor activities. The way touchscreens are used can be perceived as threatening to these traditional concepts of play and learning and parents are understandably anxious as to the consequences of this for their children's development and wellbeing. Concerns were also prevalent around the potentially negative impact of touchscreen use on babies' and toddlers' interaction and communication skills. Again, much research has highlighted the importance of talking to babies and encouraging social interaction to ensure healthy emotional and social development (see Whitehead, 2010), and touchscreen use appears to challenge this in ways documented in the parents' responses. However, there was also much positive feedback on the use of tablets to enable very young children to connect easily with distant family members via Skype or FaceTime, suggesting that it may not be touchscreen technology itself which is seen as a threat to the ideals of very early childhood, but how it is being used.

SUMMARY

This chapter has provided an overview of how some 0–3 year olds play with touchscreens, dependent on their stage of development and permitted access by parents, and has discussed ongoing debates and research pertaining to this emerging area. The findings of the online UK parental survey reported here have highlighted the growing practice of babies and toddlers using this technology as a contested space in which adults attempt to reconcile their understanding of early childhood and their role as parents in the face of 'new' technology which has the potential to both threaten and emancipate their children's experience of their earliest years of life.

Traditional discourses on childhood play and development are still clearly instrumental in influencing parental perceptions and behaviours, but there appears to be a growing recognition of previously undocumented abilities of very young children to self-direct learning and move into new territories of expression and learning using touchscreens. As one parent commented with wonder in relation to her 10-month-old son: 'I can't believe how fast he's picked things up – it really is amazing how well he can navigate a touchscreen to get what he wants.'

Given the seemingly unstoppable rise of ownership of touchscreen devices in the home environment (at least in the Western world), it is clear that there is an urgent need for more extensive research that focuses on the potential affordances and disadvantages engendered by very young children playing with touchscreens.

Useful websites

www.Childnet.com (a charity offering guidance and support to parents and teachers about how to keep children safe when using digital technology)
www.wordsforlife.org.uk (guidance on using technology with the under 5s)

References and further reading

Adams, G. (2014) The day I realised my toddler was addicted to the iPad. *Daily Mail* 29 January: 14.

Berk, L. (2012) *Child Development.* London: Pearson.

Bond, D. (2013) *Project Wild Thing.* Retrieved from: http://projectwildthing.com/ (accessed 27 January 2017).

Cocozza, P. (2014) Are iPads and tablets bad for young children? *The Guardian* 8 January: 12.

Common Sense Media (2013) *Zero to Eight: Children's Media Use in America 2013.* Retrieved from: www.commonsensemedia.org (accessed 2 December 2016).

Flewitt, R.S. (2012) Multimodal perspectives on early childhood literacies. In J. Larson and J. Marsh (eds), *The Sage Handbook of Early Childhood Literacy.* London: Sage pp. 295–310.

Formby, S. (2014) *Practitioner Perspectives: Children's Use of Technology in the Early Years.* Harlow: Pearson/National Literacy Trust. Retrieved from: www.literacytrust.org.uk/assets/0002/1135/Early_years_practitioner_report.pdf (accessed 27 January 2017).

Higonnet, A. (1998) *Pictures of Innocence: The History and Crisis of Ideal Childhood.* London: Thames & Hudson.

Hourcade, J., Mascher, S., Wu, D. and Pantoja, L. (2015) Look, my baby is using an iPad! An analysis of YouTube videos of infants and toddlers using tablets. CHI April, pp. 18–23.

House, R. (2012) The inappropriateness of ICT in early childhood: Arguments from philosophy, pedagogy and developmental research. In S. Suggate and E. Reese (eds), *Contemporary Debates in Childhood Education and Development.* Abingdon: Routledge, pp. 105–120.

Karmiloff-Smith, A. (2015) Pioneering study into whether or not babies learn from touchscreens. London: Birkbeck, University of London News website. Retrieved from: www.bbk.ac.uk/news/pioneering-study-into-whether-or-not-babies-learn-from-touchscreens (accessed 27 January 2017).

Kelly C (2013) 'Let's do some jumping together': Intergenerational participation in the use of remote technology to co-construct social relations over distance. *Journal of Early Childhood Research* 13(1): 29–46.

Kucirkova, N., Messer, D., Sheehy, K. and Flewitt, R. (2013) Sharing personalised stories on iPads: A close look at one parent–child interaction. *Literacy* 47(3): 115–122.

Louv, R. (2010) *Last Child in the Woods: Saving Our Children from Nature-Deficit Disorder*. London: Atlantic Books.

Marsh, J., Brooks, G., Hughes, J., et al. (2005) *Digital Beginnings: Young Children's Use of Popular Culture, Media and New Technologies*. Sheffield: Literacy Research Centre, University of Sheffield.

Marsh, J., Plowman, L., Yamada-Rice, D., et al. (2016) Digital play: A new classification. *Early Years* 36(3): 242–253.

Merchant, G. (2015) Keep taking the tablets: iPads, story apps and early literacy. *Australian Journal of Language and Literacy* 38(1): 3–11.

O'Connor, J. and Fotakopoulou, O. (2016) A threat to early childhood innocence or the future of learning? Parents' perspectives on the use of touchscreen technology by 0–3 year olds in the UK. *Contemporary Issues in Early Childhood* 17(2): 1–13.

Ofcom (2014) *Children and Parents: Media Use and Attitudes Report*. Retrieved from: http://stakeholders.ofcom.org.uk/binaries/research/media-literacy/media-use-attitudes-14/Childrens_2014_Report.pdf (accessed 27 January 2017).

Palaiologou I. (2016) Teachers' dispositions towards the role of digital devices in play-based pedagogy in early childhood education. *Early Years* 36(3): 305–321.

Palmer, S. (2007) *Toxic Childhood: How the Modern World is Damaging Our Children and What We Can Do About It*. London: Orion.

Patte, M. and Brown, F. (2012) *Rethinking Children's Play*. London: Bloomsbury Academic.

Radesky, J., Silverstein, M., Zuckerman, B. and Christakis, D. (2014) Infant self-regulation and early childhood media exposure. *Pediatrics* 133(5): 1172–1178.

Radesky, J., Schumacher, J. and Zuckerman, B. (2015) Mobile and interactive media use by young children: The good, the bad and the unknown. *Pediatrics* 135(1): 1–3.

US Centers for Disease Control (n.d.) *Milestone Moments*. Retrieved from: www.cdc.gov/ncbddd/actearly/pdf/parents_pdfs/milestonemomentseng508.pdf (accessed 27 January 2017).

Verenika, I. and Kervin, L. (2012) iPads, digital play and pre-schoolers. *He Kupu* 2(5): 4–16.

Vittrup, B., Snider, S., Ross, K.K. and Rippy, J. (2016) Parental perceptions of the role of media and technology in their young children's lives. *Journal of Early Childhood Research* 14(1): 43–54.

Whitehead, M. (2010) *Language and Literacy in the Early Years 0–7*. London: Sage.

Wohlwend, K. (2009) Early adopters: Playing new literacies and pretending new technologies in print-centric classrooms. *Journal of Early Childhood Literacy* 9(2): 117–140.

Yelland, N. (2015) iPlay, iLearn, iGrow: Tablet technologies, curriculum, pedagogies and learning in the 21st century. In S. Garvis and N. Lemon (eds), *Understanding Digital Technologies and Young Children: An International Perspective*. Abingdon: Routledge.

PART 3
SUPPORTING PLAYFUL PEDAGOGIES WITH TECHNOLOGIES

8

CHILDREN'S RESPONSES TO WORKING AND NON-WORKING DIGITAL TECHNOLOGIES

Jo Bird

CHAPTER OVERVIEW

In Chapter 1, Arnott considers how we define technologies in practice and in children's lives. Defining technologies in this manner is vital to our understanding of children's play with contemporary resources because it directly relates to our understanding of how children are able to incorporate 'technologies' into their play or how practitioners can utilise 'technologies' in their practice. Elsewhere in this book we see references to new types of play, i.e. 'digital play', 'technological play' as well as new pedagogies, such as 'digital pedagogies'. Without a definition of technologies in this context, we cannot take these theoretical perspectives further. In this chapter, we take an even broader perspective on defining technologies, by seeking to explore children's play with both working and non-working technologies. In early childhood settings, working technologies may include computers, iPads, still and video cameras. Non-working technologies often include previously working telephones, ex-display mobiles, keyboards and computer equipment and toys that simulate technologies. Here we are able to explore the place of technologies in traditional play scenes and to investigate how children's play is shaped by the interactivity of the resource, or the 'concept' of the resource within society.

This chapter intends to:

- Explore children's engagement with working and non-working digital technologies.
- Identify mature play skills in children's technological play.
- Understanding children's technological meaning-making.

This chapter will explore children's engagement with digital technologies in early childhood educational settings. The traditional practices in early childhood education are often seen at odds with digital technologies and therefore digital technologies are restricted and sometimes removed altogether (Lindahl and Folkesson, 2012). Children's experiences with digital technologies have been supported by parents and policy makers who view technological competencies as an essential skill for future success. This has resulted in digital technologies being viewed as 'an integral part of educational provision for young children in affluent nations' (Stephen and Plowman, 2014: 330). This chapter aims to affirm children's technological play as 'real play' with the potential to extend children's learning. Based on research conducted in two early childhood settings, the findings illustrate how children engaged with the provided digital technologies in settings that valued play as the way children learn (Wood, 2013). Changing the way children's engagement with digital technologies is viewed can help to develop new practices, which focus on the possibilities for learning with digital technologies and their potential for teaching children.

A change in perspective in relation to how digital technologies are viewed in practice must then be coupled to an understanding of how we view play in the digital era, as previously discussed in Chapter 3 by Yelland and Gilbert. Defining play is an ongoing challenge for researchers (Pellegrini, 2009; van Oers, 2012; Wood, 2010) and with the increase of digital technologies in children's lives, both in the home and educational contexts, authors are calling for a rethinking of play in the digital context. They believe technological play is children's way of enacting the practices they see occurring in their social context (Edwards, 2013; Marsh, 2010; Plowman et al., 2010b). If technological play is viewed in this way, the practices that surround the provision of digital technologies in early childhood education would support children's meaning-making attempts and value this type of play as a modern vehicle for learning. But this is not always the case. It seems the relationship between traditional play and technological play is an ongoing issue for educators, often with traditional play winning the debate.

To solidify the perspective on children's play with technologies, Yelland (1999) called for further knowledge around how children incorporate digital technologies in their play and how they can support learning, then reissued the call over a decade later (Yelland, 2011). Yet it still took another five years before we started to see documentation of children's play-based experiences emerging. This chapter adds to this evolving body of literature and explores how children engage with digital technologies in play-based ways.

Theoretical basis for technologies as tools for imaginative play

Vygotsky (1978) stated a subject needs to mediate tools in order to achieve their object of activity. By viewing technologies as tools, the children can mediate the devices in order to achieve their object of activity. In early childhood settings, play is often valued as the way children learn (Brooker, 2011; Wood, 2013) and for children, imaginative play is their object of activity.

For Vygotsky to label children's activity as play it needs to have three requirements: an imaginary situation, roles and rules related to the roles. Within the imagined situation, children behave a certain way to the requirements of the role they are taking on. The concept of separate meaning from object occurs when children can substitute one object for another (Vygotsky, 1978). Another theoretical concept present in this research project was imagination. For Vygotsky (1987) imagination is not fantasy, instead he believed imagination links to reality in four ways. The first way involves children creating a play scenario based on their real experiences. The second way is where they combine the described reality of another person in their imaginings. An example would be creating a play scenario based on their favourite storybook. While they may not have directly experienced the elements of the story, they can use these described elements in their own play. The third way links real emotions to what they imagine. Vygotsky used the example of a child imagining clothes hanging on a chair are a robber breaking into their house. The child feels real emotions but the robber is imagined. In the fourth way, children create new objects that become part of their reality and can be used in new play scenarios, in the first way. This is where imagination continues in a cycle and new building blocks for their reality are created (Edwards, 2011). The four ways of imagination illustrate how a child's experiences are broadened and how new cultural tools are created. Using a cultural-historical framework and Vygotsky's ideas of play and mediation, the following research study aimed to explore the children's use of digital technologies as tools in their imaginative play.

Exploring children's engagement with working and non-working digital technologies

This section is based on research from a PhD study (Bird, 2016) involving children from two early childhood settings situated in middle-class suburbs of Melbourne, Australia. The ethnographic study aimed to explore children's use of working and non-working technologies and the educators' provision of these devices. Prior to the commencement of the study, educators were asked which working and non-working digital technologies were available in their setting. The non-working digital technologies provided included toys that simulate digital technologies and broken, unpowered or no longer working devices for the children's use. These devices were placed in imaginative play spaces both inside the classroom and in the outside area. The working digital technologies provided in the two settings included still and video cameras, interactive toys, computers and iPads. These devices needed educators to turn them on and select the apps and programs the children could access. The educators also imposed a range of rules and restrictions surrounding their use, which included time limits, one child at a time, or limiting their use to rainy days only. Data were collected through observations, photographs and video footage of the children engaged with digital technologies in their play. Data were deductively coded (LeCompte, 2012) to working and non-working technologies and then to the theoretical concepts of Vygotsky's (1978) play requirements (imaginary situation, roles and rules), separating meaning from object and the four ways of imagination (Vygotsky, 1987).

While there were differences in what was provided and the rules and restrictions surrounding their provision in the two centres, the ways in which the children engaged with the available digital technologies were the same. The findings showed that the children engaged with the non-working digital technologies in three ways. In the first way, the children *accepted* the provided digital technologies and used them in their play scenario. In the second way, if the technology was not provided, the children *represented* the technology they needed and used it in their play. In the third way, if the technology was not available the children responded by *creating* the technology they needed for their play.

In the following sections I will demonstrate how children engaged with working and non-working technologies in six ways, as shown in Table 8.1.

Table 8.1   Engagement with working and non-working technologies.

	Engagement
Non-working technology	**Accept** – Using device as represented in society
	Represent – Using another object to substitute for the needed technology
	Create – To create the needed technology
Working technology	**Accept** – Using device as provided by the educator
	Negotiate – To negotiate the rules and restrictions to meet their play needs
	Abandon – To abandon the device and their play plans

Non-working digital technologies

In traditional play spaces, children were given opportunities and encouraged to enact the cultural practices they witness in their everyday lives, with props and experiences set up to support imaginative play. Their experiences with digital technologies were no different. Educators set up imaginative play spaces, like home corner, pretend hospitals or shops, and scaffolded the children's learning within these scenarios. The technological props added to these spaces included telephones for parents to make calls, computers for the doctors to type notes and cash registers to tally up a customer's purchases. While these behaviours may reflect the practices of years gone by, the behaviours children enacted incorporated the contemporary behaviours they are exposed to. These play behaviours included taking a photograph and uploading it to Facebook, searching an iPad for a recipe to cook in the home corner kitchen or pretending to play games on a non-working mobile.

Working Technologies

Two computers were available at the first centre, Cosmic Kindergarten, for the children's free play. At the second, Creative Kindergarten, computers were only available for children's free play on rainy days. At both centres iPads were restricted in the ways they were provided. Creative Kindergarten allowed children's free play on the iPad during rainy day sessions, whereas the iPads were not available for children's free play at Cosmic Kindergarten. Both centres used the iPads for playing music and stories, but the children were not allowed to watch the screen and the educators often redirected children or turned the iPad over to enforce this restriction. Still cameras were used by the educators to document children's learning and were rarely available for the children's use.

How the children engaged with the working digital technologies depended on the programs and apps available on each device. Programs and apps that encourage creativity and allow children to deviate from a set script result in children being more engaged and for longer periods of time (Yelland and Gilbert, 2013). The findings illustrated that the children engaged with the working digital technologies in three ways. The first way children engaged with the working digital technologies was to *accept* the digital technologies and use them how the educators planned. The second way children engaged with the working digital technologies was to *negotiate* the rules surrounding the provision of the working digital technologies. The third way the children engaged with the working digital technologies was to *abandon* their play plans.

Mature play skills with working and non-working technologies

This section provides examples of how children demonstrated each of the ways in which they engaged with technologies (see Table 8.1) but goes further to describe how elements of these examples demonstrate children's mature play skills with technologies.

Non-working digital technologies – accept

Both centres provided non-working digital technologies for children to use in their imaginative play. The children *accepted* these and created play scenarios that involved technological behaviours that were imitations of what they experience in their everyday lives. In the first case study, Vygotsky's (1978) play requirements of the imaginary situation, roles and rules were evident in Ellen and Hannah's play in the hospital scene.

CASE STUDY 1   HANNAH, 4 AND ELLEN, 5

At Cosmic Kindergarten, the home corner space had been changed to a hospital. There were many props available to create the hospital including: a bed, a table with a non-working laptop and phones, paper and pens, white lab coats, syringes, stethoscopes, paper hats, plastic gloves, bandages and medicine bottles. Hannah and Ellen pretended they were a doctor and a mother. As they swapped roles they also swapped props: the doctor wore the gloves and the mother used the non-working mobile. Ellen gave Hannah a phone stating, 'This is the doctor's phone. So Mum can call the doctor.'

Ellen extended the play by giving the doctor a phone. This allowed the play to be more realistic, as the doctor needed a phone to answer when the mother called.

In early childhood, it is argued that children learn from hands-on experiences with objects and through the interactions they have with the peers and educators. From a cultural-historical view, children learn from hands on experiences with objects and through the interactions they have with the peers and educators (van Oers, 2013). This cultural-historical view of play positions children's learning as a cultural apprenticeship (Rogoff, 1990). This apprenticeship prepares children to be active members of and to contribute to the society in which they live. Part of children's cultural learning involves mastering the cultural tools existing in their community. Children work towards mastering cultural tools through play, which is their way to make meaning of what they witness in their outside experiences.

In the next case study, Lisa pretended to be a working mother. Based on her home experiences of her own mother, Lisa moved between the practices around caring for a baby and working on a laptop. Lisa's cultural apprenticeship is displayed through her learning to master the laptop and achieve her object of activity – being a working mother.

CASE STUDY 2   LISA, 5

Lisa has a baby brother and her mother works from home as a sales consultant for a kitchen appliance company. At home, Lisa often observes her mother feeding her brother while she works on her laptop in her office. During one particular kindergarten session, Lisa sat at a non-working laptop in the home corner. She had a baby in one arm and typed with the other. There was a non-working mobile on the table next to the laptop that she used on and off throughout her play. Lisa moved around home corner to collect items she needed for the baby (blanket, highchair, bowl and spoon), then returned to the laptop and continued typing. She placed the baby in the highchair and the bowl and spoon on the tray of the highchair. She looked back at the laptop and typed. She pretended the mobile rang, picked it up and talked into it. She returned it to the table. She moved between feeding the baby and typing.

Both of these examples of children's play showed how the non-working digital technologies supported children's ability to enact the behaviours and practices from their everyday lives. The children were also practising their possible future roles in society, Ellen and Hannah were doctors and a mother and Lisa a mother and computer worker (Wood, 2013). Children's play reflects their everyday experiences and the changes in behaviours seen in children's play can be attributed to the changes in wider society. From a cultural-historical perspective, changes in children's play represents an adjustment to the skills and knowledge needed for the particular context at a particular time (Edwards, 2013).

Non-working digital technologies – represent

Children often substitute objects for the props they need in their play. Vygotsky (1978) described this concept as separating meaning from object and the children displayed this concept when they used an object to represent the technology they needed for their play. Separating meaning from object is where children act differently to what they see or they use an object to substitute another (Vygotsky, 1978). According to Bodrova and Leong (2007), this is a mature play skill that demonstrates the children's developing symbolic functioning.

CASE STUDY 3   YASMINE, 5 AND AMY, 4

Sitting on the floor, Yasmine and Amy were building with construction blocks. Yasmine picked up a block, held it to her ear pretending it was a mobile to talk to Amy. Amy picked up another block and pretended to answer Yasmine's call.

In this example, both Yasmine and Amy were able to separate meaning from object when they used blocks as mobiles to talk to each other. This concept is extended when children can describe the objects or actions, rather than needing to rely on a physical object or to act out a particular behaviour (Leong and Bodrova, 2012). An example of this was when another child, Maria, used her hand as a mobile while playing outside and rather than interrupt her play to find a non-working mobile.

Non-working digital technologies – create

When the digital technologies provided did not meet the children's needs, they *created* what they needed, often in the pasting area. This was dependent on the children's imagination and creativity skills. The educators supported and encouraged this behaviour through providing the materials they needed to make their technologies.

CASE STUDY 4   JOSHUA, 4

In the pasting area, Joshua created a video camera out of boxes. He asked Madeleine if he could record her playing with the play dough. He stood back and said 'Action!' as he held up his video camera. When he finished, he said to Madeleine 'Thanks. That was awesome.' He then moved on to record something else.

In the above case study, Joshua displayed all four ways of imagination in his play with a video camera (Vygotsky, 1987). For example, he used his own knowledge of video cameras, including what he had been told about using video cameras, he displayed a range of real emotions and he created a video camera to use in his play. This example showed Joshua had play skills of a complex level. He used his created video camera to initiate interactions with his friends and establish joint play scenarios. The play around his created video camera not only continued until the end of the kindergarten session but continued and was extended over several weeks. Bodrova and Leong (2007) believe that children's play themes that extend across multiple days exhibit advanced play by 'requiring more self-regulation, planning and memory' (p. 143). Joshua's educators also encouraged the play to continue across several days through offering him a place to store his camera so he could access it for future play.

Working digital technologies – accept

The first way children engaged with the working digital technologies was to accept and use them as their educator provided them. The following case study shows Wade engaged with a drawing and painting program called Tux Paint (New Breed Software, 2002).

CASE STUDY 5   WADE, 4

Using Tux Paint, Wade created an underwater scene. He coloured in the seaweed and the plants. He added stamps of fish and sharks. He told a story related to his drawing, describing what he was doing as he went.

The Tux Paint program was open-ended and allowed Wade to be creative. His imaginative play involved the story he created and the characters available in the program acted out the story. Wade displayed play that is commonly seen with miniature animals in imaginative play experiences in early childhood settings. The difference here was Wade created his play scenario with digital characters and the story portrayed on a screen.

Working digital technologies – negotiate

The second way children engaged with the working digital technologies was to *negotiate* the rules surrounding their provision. Educators enforce restrictions including time limits, turn-taking and one child on the device at a time, that all influence how children could engage with the digital technologies. Children responded by negotiating these rules and restrictions in order to use the digital technologies for their play in the way they wanted.

CASE STUDY 6   CHRISTIAN, 6

When the iPad was being used to play 'Everything is Awesome' from *The Lego Movie* (Miller and Lord, 2014), Christian selected a different song. He used his thumb to scroll through the other YouTube videos. He selected one but it took ages to buffer. He picked a different app to play. Other children joined him and gave their suggestions of what to play.

In the above case study, Christian negotiated the rules by not only engaging with the iPad on a non-rainy day but also by selecting a game rather than the music that the iPad was provided for. Christian was a competent user of the iPad and could explain to the other children that their chosen app was taking a long time to 'buffer'. A conversation between the children then ensued around their home iPad use and the favourite apps. This behaviour was not recognised or extended at the kindergarten; instead their home iPad use was ignored.

Working digital technologies – abandon

There were times when the children could not engage with the digital technologies in the way they wanted to, so they abandoned their play. This occurred more often than was captured as data. Knowing the rules for the working technologies, the children did not ask to use the devices because they knew the answer would by no. When the educators imposed the rules and restrictions they often focused on the technology rather than the activity the children were engaged in.

CASE STUDY 7   JAYDEN, 4

Jayden took the iPad off the shelf and sat down with it in his lap. He scrolled through the apps and selected one saying, 'I know this one.' He used both hands to press the screen. Other children sat around him and watched. Louise, an educator, came over and said, 'Come on Jayden, it's too nice today' as she removed the iPad from his hands.

In the example above, Louise removed the iPad from Jayden resulting in Jayden abandoning his play. If Louise observed the behaviours that were occurring around the iPad, including the cooperation, social interactions and communication, all valued skills in early childhood education (Leong and Bodrova, 2012), she may have used the children's interest in the iPad to extend their engagement and learning. Instead, Louise focused on the rules around iPad use and stopped Jayden's activity. Jayden responded to the interruption to his play with aimless wandering around the kindergarten environment.

Discussion: Technological meaning-making

Children experience many technology-related practices in their daily activities and they re-enact these experiences in their play. Their use of digital technologies in the home context is extensive, where they have already developed a range of technological competencies (McPake et al., 2013). When they attend their early childhood setting what the digital technologies can afford them is limited due to the rules and restrictions educators impose. Despite educator claims that the curriculum is based 'on children's lived experience of their home, community, and early childhood education settings', digital technologies are not provided in ways that support children's imaginative play and learning (Edwards et al., 2015: 73).

The educators positioned the working digital technologies and play as two opposing forces, with only rare examples where the two merged. The literature provides examples of young children who merge the two. One example is O'Mara and Laidlow's (2011) description of the sisters engaged in a tea party with dolls, teddies and an iPad. They seamlessly move from the iPad app to their real toys and tea set (see p. 115 for more information). Edwards (2013) views children's ability to see themselves embodied in the avatar on the screen as 'sophisticated' play which clearly displays their ability to separate meaning from object (p. 204). These examples of the blending of real and virtual support the need to reconceptualise play in relation to digital technologies (see for example, Goldstein, 2011; Marsh, 2010; Plowman et al., 2010a).

The children and educators had different perceptions of what digital technologies could afford in a play-based setting. The difference between the children's and the educators' technological knowledge created a divide where the children were advancing in-step with society's technological understandings and the educators remained stuck in their traditional beliefs and practices of a time when digital technologies were not so prevalent. The children saw the computer and iPad as important to their play and learning, whereas the educators saw them as 'a special treat to be used on rainy days' (educator interview). Yelland and Gilbert (2013: 1) recommend that 'the pedagogical repertoires of teachers and carers need to be extended' so they include digital technologies regularly in children's daily experiences. The first step is knowledge around how children engage with the various digital technologies, so educators can provide them in ways that support children's play and cultural meaning-making.

The educators supported children's play with non-working digital technologies. This was the extent to which children's play with non-working digital technologies aligned with the educators' current understandings of play. The educators focused on the children's play and what was occurring rather than the technology involved. By focusing on the play, the educators already had the pedagogical strategies that support children's play and learning and these practices came naturally to the educators. What did not come naturally were the conceptual understandings related to the digital technologies. For example, understanding the workings of Facebook or the specific iPad apps children referred to. When working digital technologies were provided for children's free play, educators focused on the digital technologies rather than the possible play the digital technologies could support. This focus was illustrated in the rules and restrictions educators imposed and the value they placed on children's activities with the working digital technologies.

The provision of the working digital technologies were influenced by the educators' knowledge and understanding of the different devices, the training they had around how to support children's play with working digital technologies, and their pedagogical beliefs around the potential for children's learning with digital technologies. Both research educators had limited training in how to provide digital technologies for children's play and learning. Nuttall et al. (2015) believe current professional development around digital technologies focuses on *what* to provide instead of *how* to provide it. Training needs to support educators' pedagogical understandings of digital technologies in early childhood education, and then educators can use the digital technologies in ways that support children's meaning-making and learning. It is not the device that promotes children's learning but how the educators use the device to support the learning that is important (Radesky et al., 2015).

The choice of the programs and apps educators provided on the computers and iPads also influenced how children could engage with them. Many apps that are categorised as 'educational' focus on 'drill-and-practice' and do not allow the children to be creative or deviate from a set script (Goodwin and Highfield, 2012: 2). When apps are open-ended they allow for children's creativity, problem solving and they encourage 'engagement with ideas and deep learning' (Yelland and Gilbert, 2013: 1).

SUMMARY

The apps and computer programs provided need to be open-ended and encourage children's creativity, problem solving and deep learning. (Yelland and Gilbert, 2013). This chapter has described children's engagement with digital technologies in play-based settings. Children encounter digital technologies in all areas of their daily lives and their early childhood setting should be no different. Technological competency and play to support learning are both valued concepts in early childhood education. Through understanding how children engage with digital technologies in play, educators can support this meaning-making and create positive outcomes for children's technological play and learning.

References and further reading

Bird, J. (2016) *'It's All Pretend.' Exploring the Engagement and Provision of Working and Non-working Technologies in Play-based Settings.* Paper presented at the Australian Assoication for Research in Education (AARE), 27 November – 1st December, Melbourne, Australia.

Bodrova, E. and Leong, D. (2007) *Tools of the Mind: The Vygotskian Approach to Early Childhood Education*, 2nd edn. Upper Saddle River, NJ: Pearson Education.

Brooker, L. (2011) Taking children seriously: An alternative agenda for research? *Journal of Early Childhood Research* 9(2): 137–149.

Edwards, S. (2011) Lessons from a really useful engine: Using Thomas the Tank Engine to examine the relationship between children's play as a leading activity, imagination and reality in children's contemporary play worlds. *Cambridge Journal of Education* 41(2): 195–210.

Edwards, S. (2013) Digital play in the early years: A contextual response to the problem of integrating technologies and play-based pedagogies in the early childhood curriculum. *European Early Childhood Education Research Journal* 21(2): 199–212.

Edwards, S., Nuttall, J., Mantilla, A., et al. (2015) Digital play: What do early childhood teachers see? In S. Bulfin, N. Johnson and C. Bigum (eds), *Critical Perspectives on Technology and Education.* New York: Palgrave Macmillan, pp. 69–84.

Goldstein, J. (2011) Technology and play. In A. Pellegrini (ed.), *The Oxford Handbook of the Development of Play.* New York: Oxford University Press pp. 322–340.

Goodwin, K. and Highfield, K. (2012) iTouch and iLearn: An examination of 'educational' apps. Paper presented at the Early Education and Technology for Children Conference, 14–16 March, Salt Lake City, UT.

LeCompte, M.D. (2012) *Analysis and Interpretation of Ethnographic Data: A Mixed Method Approach*, 2nd edn. Lanham, MD: AltaMira Press.

Leong, D. and Bodrova, E. (2012) Assessing and scaffolding make-believe play. *Young Children* 67(1): 28–34.

Lindahl, M.G. and Folkesson, A.-M. (2012) ICT in preschool: Friend or foe? The significance of norms in a changing practice. *International Journal of Early Years Education* 20(4): 422–436.

Marsh, J. (2010) Young children's play in online virtual worlds. *Journal of Early Childhood Research* 8(1): 23–39.

McPake, J., Plowman, L. and Stephen, C. (2013) Pre-school children creating and communicating with digital technologies in the home. *British Journal of Educational Technology* 44(3): 421–431.

Miller, C. and Lord, P. (writers) (2014) *The Lego Movie*. Producers R. Lee and D. Lin. Warner Bros.

New Breed Software (2002) Tux Paint [computer program]. Retrieved from: www.tuxpaint.org (accessed 27 January 2017).

Nuttall, J., Edwards, S., Mantilla, A., Grieshaber, S. and Wood, E. (2015) The role of motive objects in early childhood teacher development concerning children's digital play and play-based learning in early childhood curricula. *Professional Development in Education* 41(2): 222–235.

O'Mara, J. and Laidlaw, L. (2011) Living in the iworld: Two literacy researchers reflect on the changing texts and literacy practices of childhood. *English Teaching: Practice and Critique* 10(4): 149–159. Retrieved from: http://edlinked.soe.waikato.ac.nz/research/journal/view.php?view=true&id=62&p=1 (accessed 27 January 2017).

Pellegrini, A. (2009) *The Role of Play in Human Development*. New York: Oxford University Press.

Plowman, L., McPake, J. and Stephen, C. (2010a) The technologisation of childhood? Young children and technology in the home. *Children and Society* 24(1): 63–74.

Plowman, L., Stephen, C. and McPake, J. (2010b) *Growing Up with Technology: Young Children Learning in a Digital World*. Abingdon: Routledge.

Radesky, J.S., Schumacher, J. and Zuckerman, B. (2015) Mobile and interactive media use by young children: The good, the bad, and the unknown. *Pediatrics* 135(1): 1–3.

Rogoff, B. (1990) *Apprenticeship in Thinking*. New York: Oxford University Press.

Stephen, C. and Plowman, L. (2014) Digital play. In L. Brooker, M. Blaise and S. Edwards (eds), *The Sage Handbook of Play and Learning in Early Childhood*. Los Angeles, CA: Sage, pp. 330–341.

van Oers, B. (2012) Culture in play. In J. Valsiner (ed.), *The Oxford Handbook of Culture and Psychology*. New York: Oxford University Press, pp. 936–956.

Van Oers, B. (2013) An activity theory view on the development of play. In I. Schousboe and D. Winther-Lindqvist (eds), *Children's Play and Development. Cultural-Historical Perspectives* Dordrecht, Netherlands: Springer, pp. 231–249.

Vygotsky, L.S. (1978) *Mind in Society: The Development of Higher Psychological Processes*. Cambridge, MA: Harvard University Press.

Vygotsky, L.S. (1987) Imagination and its development in childhood. Trans. N. Minick. In R.W. Rieber and A.S. Carton (eds), *The Collected Works of L.S. Vygotsky*, Vol. 1. New York: Plenum Press, pp. 339–349.

Wohlwend, K.E. (2009) Early adopters: Playing new literacies and pretending new technologies in print-centric classrooms. *Journal of Early Childhood Literacy* 9(2): 117–140.

Wood, E. (2010) Reconceptualizing the play–pedaogoy relationship. From control to complexity. In L. Brooker and S. Edwards (eds), *Engaging Play*. Maidenhead: Open University Press, pp. 11–24.

Wood, E. (2013) *Play, Learning and the Early Childhood Curriculum*, 3rd edn. Los Angeles, CA: Sage.

Wood, E. (2014) The play–pedagogy interface in contemporary debates. In L. Brooker, M. Blaise and S. Edwards (eds), *The Sage Handbook of Play and Learning in Early Childhood*. Los Angeles: Sage, pp. 145–156.

Yelland, N. (1999) Technology as play. *Early Childhood Education Journal* 26(4): 217–220.

Yelland, N. (2011) Reconceptualising play and learning in the lives of young children. *Australasian Journal of Early Childhood* 36: 4–12. Retrieved from: www.earlychildhood australia.org.au/our-publications/australasian-journal-early-childhood/ajec-archive (accessed 27 January 2017).

Yelland, N. and Gilbert, C. (2013) *iPlay, iLearn, iGrow*. Commissioned research report for IBM. Melbourne. Retrieved from: www.ipadsforeducation.vic.edu.au/userfiles/files/IBM %20Report%20iPlay,%20iLearn%20&%20iGrow.pdf (accessed 27 January 2017).

9

DIGITAL PEDAGOGY: HOW TEACHERS SUPPORT DIGITAL PLAY IN THE EARLY YEARS

Marilyn Fleer

CHAPTER OVERVIEW

Children are increasingly embedded in environments where digital technologies create new conditions for learning and development (McKenney and Voogt, 2010). We know a lot about children's experiences (e.g. Saçkes et al., 2011) and teacher perspectives (e.g. Hinostroza et al., 2013) where new approaches for supporting children's engagement with digital devices have emerged (see Wohlwend, 2015). This growing body of research gives a foundation for knowing about how digital devices are used by teachers and by children. However, less is known about the type of pedagogy that is needed to support children's play and learning with digital devices in the early years. In drawing upon a cultural-historical conceptualisation of research (Vygotsky, 1997), this chapter seeks to:

- Introduce the concept of *digital pedagogy.*
- Present three case studies which show the relations between teacher pedagogy and children's engagement with digital technology.
- Highlight children's perspectives when children make slowmation animations.

The chapter begins with a brief discussion of the literature to give a backdrop for discussing *digital pedagogy.* This is followed by three case studies that present the stories of children and teachers engaged with digital technologies. Fairytales are used in each context to frame the digital experiences of the children. At the conclusion to each case study there is a discussion on the special nature of the pedagogy that was used by the teachers; and finally, an analysis of the children's perspective is featured in relation to the *digital pedagogy* used by each of the teachers.

Digital contexts in the early years for supporting play and learning

Three types of digital contexts emerge in the literature. They are: (1) toys with computer chips; (2) tangibles (touchscreen devices); and (3) the diversity of apps (or computer games). It is suggested that recently available digital devices create new play and learning conditions (Wohlwend, 2015) that we are still to understand from the perspective of the child (Nolan and McBride, 2014). For example, 'Digital toys can serve as catalysts for new forms of play and can have a positive influence on the content of more traditional forms of play' (Kjällander and Moinian, 2014: 29). The new play and learning conditions are also discussed by Moore (2014), who gives an example to illustrate the similarities rather than differences between digital and non-digital forms of play and learning:

> Students' manipulation of digital paintbrush, magnets, and crayons, or their tapping of simulated water represent their engagement in 'as if' behaviors – it is 'as if' they are painting or tapping at fish. However, they are merely manipulating pixilated lights and colors rather than real, liquid paint, or wet water. Their experimentations and creations are real and yet not real – just as a baby doll is simultaneously real and yet not real. In both instances the child must agree that the objects at hand represent something not present – the cloth and plastic represent a real baby, and the pixilated, colored lights represent paint. (Moore, 2014: 253–254)

What Moore (2014) draws attention to is how the new forms of play and learning arise, creating new conditions in virtual worlds but also the everyday play of children. Another rich example of this is given by O'Mara and Laidlaw (2011), who describe a 21st-century tea party (as also referred to in Chapter 8):

> *The transformation of objects inside the dramatic play seamlessly shifts from the virtual to the physical, the cups of tea being served, drunk and spilled in the virtual iPad space extending over into the pouring of 'cups of tea' served from the teapot into the plastic tea set on the other side of the picnic blanket. The boundaries between 'physical' and 'virtual' blur, with all play objects – the iPad, stuffed toys, plastic tea-set – crossing into the realm of imagination and the narrative structures of dramatic playing inside a virtual world.* (O'Mara and Laidlaw, 2011: 150; original emphasis)

The blending of on-screen and off-screen play has also been noted by Verenikina and Kervin (2011), where some software gives rise to social pretend play, drawing further attention to the complexity of play and learning in digital contexts. Conceptualising on-screen and off-screen activities has also been considered by Marsh (2014), who when researching how children engaged with virtual games, such as Club Penguin, put forward the categories of offline/online as markers for distinguishing between time when children were using virtual games on the internet, and when not engaged in internet use. This is also evident in the research of Talamo et al. (2009), who note that children are simultaneously in the digital world and everyday practices constructing and maintaining social networks across both platforms.

We also know from the relevant literature that children engage in new practices when using digital devices, such as touches, swipes, sensory or multimodal layers of interaction, as they engage in social interactions and negotiations with other children, either online or elsewhere (Wohlwend, 2015). For instance, when children use digital puppetry they are engaged in creating sound effects and dragging, resizing, narrating and animating puppet characters as they virtually interact with others.

What these studies suggest is that, *digital play* amplifies the need for children to work more consciously with the rules and roles designed into apps, thus creating new possibilities for complex play. Digital placeholders, when acting as pivots in virtual and/or augmented imaginary situations, can give a new sense to a situation, thus affording a new imaginary situation that meshes both the culturally constructed physical world and the virtual world (Fleer, 2014).

These brief examples of relevant empirical data taken from the literature show the porous nature of play and learning across virtual and real-world contexts, suggesting that digital technologies cannot be discussed independently from the general play and learning of children.

With this conceptualisaton in mind, this chapter seeks to present a discussion on the nature of *digital pedagogy* where the affordances of technologies are discussed in the context of the children's perspective and teachers' practices.

A cultural-historical conception of how teachers support digital play in the early years: Three case examples

In this section are three case examples that present the story of children and teachers from three different early years settings in Australia. The case studies were drawn from a study of children's play and learning of science where iPads and slowmation software (Hoban and Nielsen, 2014) were used by teachers to create new conditions for children's development. The study was funded by the Australian Research Council (Discovery Grant Scheme) and had full ethics approval for documenting teachers' everyday teaching practices when using digital devices with their children. The use of iPads and slowmation was new to the teachers involved in the study, and as such, they each participated in professional development and received ongoing support with the use of the digital devices and software.

The teachers were invited to select a fairytale that they could use to frame the science learning in the centres, and for the creation of a slowmation. Slowmation is abbreviated from 'slow animation' and refers to a simplified form of stop-motion animation that children use to make an animation that is played slowly at two frames per second (see the website at www.slowmation.com for examples of slowmations created by preschool and primary children). The teachers practised making a slowmation and engaged in role-playing their chosen fairytales, as part of their professional development. In addition, the teachers were supported to think about the science learning that could be fostered through the role-play and associated activities surrounding the fairytale. A cultural-historical conception of play was introduced to broaden the teachers' thinking about play (Vygotsky, 1966) and learning (Vygosky, 1987).

Data gathering consisted of video observations of the children and teachers over an extended period of time using two and sometimes three cameras in order to follow the children. The age profile of the children, and details of the amount of video observations made are shown in Table 9.1 below.

Table 9.1   Overview of sample and data generated.

Centre	Number of teachers	Number of children	Age range	Observation period	Data generated
Centre A	3	53	3.3–4.4; mean age of 3.8 years	8 weeks	242 hours
Centre B	2	20	4.6–5.7; mean age of 5.0 years	5 weeks	55 hours
Centre C	1	30	3.3–5.3; mean of 4.2 years	3 weeks	74 hours

The teachers

Five of the teachers in the study were of European heritage background, and one was of Asian descent. Each teacher was credentialed with an early childhood qualification, and used the national curriculum framework (DEEWR, 2009) for planning for learning. Each teacher provided a play-based programme.

The children

The children were drawn from families of European heritage, Asian heritage and African heritage backgrounds. This range is typical for the regions in which each of the early years settings are located.

Data analysis

Analysis of the overall data was undertaken in relation to the pedagogical practices of the teachers in the context of children's engagement with the digital devices. The study drew upon Hedegaard's (2012) *holistic conception of children's development* and Vygotsky's (1994) concept of the *social situation of development*. Vygotsky (1994) introduced the idea of how three children in exactly the same situation can experience the same event completely differently, based on their social situation of development. For example, when two children are greeted with a spider in their play environment (real or virtual), it is possible that two quite different reactions and learning possibilities could result. For instance, one child who is frightened by the spider may freeze and become stressed, while another child may be curious and observe the spider for extended periods, potentially studying its movements and behaviours, and developing great insights. Both children are in the same situation, but each experiences the event differently. The concept of the social situation of development helps explain in research the differing perspectives of children in the same event.

Hedegaard's (2012) holistic model of child development captures the child's perspective, but only in the context of the institutional perspective and societal perspective. That is, how a child experiences any event is based on the conditions and practices set up in the institutions that a child attends, such as early years settings, family homes and community activities or clubs. The practices of the early years settings determine what may be possible for a child, such as when a teacher delivers their programme, or the rules of how to behave in early years settings, such as putting up your hand to speak. The societal perspective focuses on the valued practices and goals for the institutions that a child attends, such as national curriculum, funding models and the like. The child's institutional and societal perspectives are all inter-related. How the child experiences any activity is based on both the institutional practices and societal values and cultural beliefs of that community/country.

The concepts of a holistic model of child development and the social situation of development together supported the analysis where the children's perspectives in digital contexts were being determined.

These theoretical concepts were used to examine the child's perspective in the context of the pedagogical practices of the teachers who were using digital tools to support their play and learning. The case studies that follow are illustrative of the findings, and are presented from the perspective of the teachers and the perspective of the children – as a relational whole.

CASE STUDY 1   *GOLDILOCKS AND THE THREE BEARS*

The children are aged between 3.3 and 4.4 years. They attend a childcare centre that operates each day from 8.00 a.m. to 5.00 p.m. The teachers introduced the children to the fairytale of *Goldilocks and the Three Bears* by reading, role-playing and creating a slowmation of the fairytale. The children were provided with props in the home corner to use as part of the play-based programme, and these same props were used for both group time storytelling and role-play, and for the imagination table where the iPad was eventually placed for children to create a slowmation of the story. The imagination table was set up initially for the children to simply role-play the fairytale, then over the eight weeks of data gathering, an iPad was introduced. Two examples of interactions are presented below. The first example took place early on in the eight-week period when the teachers were still new to using an iPad. The second example was taken towards the end of the eight-week period, after the researchers had been supporting the teachers for an extended period.

Example 1: The iPad

It is the free play period in the centre and the children are spread across the indoor area using all of the available resources. A small group of children are using the blocks, and several other children are roaming close by. The teacher has just received the iPad and been asked to use it with the children. The teacher is holding it in one hand, while seated on a chair near the block area. Two children approach the teacher and say, 'What's that doing?' as they point to the apps on the iPad screen. The teacher responds by saying, 'I know, I haven't got anything in them, it's just the pictures.' The child points and says, '... these just pictures?' The children move closer to the teacher, and touch the iPad, as the teacher says '... and there's no games'. The children respond by asking, 'and there's no movies too ... and only my iPad has it, and it has internet.' The teacher says, 'This is just for us at work so it has not got any movies in there.' The second child says, 'My iPad's got movies and games.' In response to the teacher asking if everyone has iPads at home, a third child says, 'Me too. I've got an iPad ...', as the child explains the details of a game and the levels, discussing the difficulty levels.

The teacher later that week uses the iPad to take photographs of what the children are doing and use the images gathered for the parent newsletter. The teacher continues to walk around holding the iPad, and when she observes interesting and purposeful (for her programme) learning, play and development, she captures this on the iPad. The children are not given the iPad to use.

Teacher perspective

The introduction of the iPad featured the teacher holding tightly onto the technology, and deflecting the children's curiosities and enquiries. She did not release the technology to the children – despite being asked to allow the children to use the equipment. The technology was viewed as precious, something that the children could not yet handle in their everyday activities in the centre. The lack of trustworthiness of the children with the technology was featured, and potentially some teacher insecurity.

Children's perspectives

Through the children's questions of the teacher, it was clear that the children not only had prior experience of using iPads, recognising it immediately, but also understood the purpose and possibilities of the technology. The children knew that the digital device would have apps, and that it could be connected to the internet, affording a range of possibilities. The children demonstrated a level of familiarity through the questions they asked, and as the broader data showed, brought to the slowmation understandings and skills about how to confidently and effectively navigate around the iPad.

We now turn to the latter observation period.

Example 2: A slowmation of *Goldilocks and the Three Bears*

The children and the teachers are seated in a circle on the carpet area for group time. The children are each given a musical instrument to hold and later play. Projected on to the wall is the slowmation animation of *Goldilocks and the Three Bears* that the children have previously created. The purpose of the group time is to re-tell the story, while looking at the projected animation, and to create a 'digital soundtrack' and narrative of the fairytale to record over the animation to make 'their

(Continued)

(Continued)

movie', as explained by the teacher: 'Have a look at the wall. Can you all see the movie on the wall? This is the story we have made of *Goldilocks and the Three Bears*. We are going to make the music for it. You know how when you watch a movie ... So we have to watch the movie whilst we make the movie.'

Teacher perspective

The teacher with now many weeks of experience of either observing the researchers work with the children to make a slowmation or by making a slowmation with a small group of children, now positions the children and herself more confidently. She uses the familiar term 'movie' to help the children to conceptualise holistically the task of making a slowmation. She also creates a group context for making the animation in a way that is meaningful to the children, as the children bring to the 'movie' the familiar narrative of the fairytale.

Children's perspectives

The children work collectively to 're-tell the story' through the use of musical instruments. Musical instruments unite the children as a collective with the same purpose of preparing the musical sound track and voiceover as the teacher narrates the fairytale. This approach allows the children to feel a part of the technical process of making a voiceover and contributing to the narrative, even though they do not re-tell the fairytale themselves. The collective approach allows all the children to make their movie, even if this could not be easily achieved by a single child. The children have agency as they shape and are shaped by this experience.

What is evident across the two examples is how the teacher's broadened technological understandings and competence created different conditions for the children, which in turn gave them new possibilities and opportunities for doing something new, such as 'making movies'. During the making of the slowmation, the children also brought their prior experiences of iPad technology, as noted in the first example, to the task and later when given the iPads, confidently navigated their way around the apps. Even though the task of making a slowmation was new to the children, their easy engagement with the digital device meant that they worked purposefully. Taken together, the children were afforded more opportunities when the teacher trusted that the children could use the technology.

We now turn to another case study where a more detailed account of making a slowmation is presented.

CASE STUDY 2   *THE THREE BILLY GOATS GRUFF*

Two teachers and a group of children aged 4.6–5.7 were followed over a five-week period as they used iPads and props to create an animation of *The Three Billy Goats Gruff*. The teachers initially used a storyboard approach to map with the children the different phases of the fairytale. One of the activities in the centre was the creation of bridges from scrap wood. One of the bridges made by the children was placed on the imagination table where plastic goats were provided and a troll. In addition, the teachers also role-played the fairytale with the children, digitally recording their role-play, which was then used as the 'voiceover' for the slowmation animation.

Two children (Alison and Timmy) and their teacher are positioned next to the iPad which is standing on a table and directed to the imagination table where a wooden bridge and plastic figures are available for the children's use to re-tell the fairytale of *The Three Billy Goats Gruff*.

Alison is positioned in front of the scene as Timmy says, 'Let's go' to signal to her to come back to the iPad and press the camera switch. Alison responds by saying as she moves back to the camera, 'Now ... and press it, yeah ... waiting' in order to ensure that Timmy does not press the button until she is out of the scene. Timmy, who is anticipating the next part of the storytelling to be captured on the iPad, says, 'Get the troll out ... I said get the troll.' Alison responds by positioning the troll under the bridge, but playfully signals to Timmy to wait before pressing the button on the iPad camera.

The two children coordinate their actions as they take photos of the props, moving them slightly, before taking another photo. The teacher holds the iPad steady as the children press the button, and she also provides support to the children by prompting them when needed. However, the children mostly coordinate their actions and direct each other to re-present the fairytale as a slowmation. A high level of intersubjectivity between the children and the technology is evident (Fleer, 2017).

Teacher perspectives

The teacher specifically positions herself as a support – physically and conceptually. She physically holds the iPad to stop if from falling over when the children press the camera button. She conceptually supports the children by being in close proximity as the children re-tell the story through moving the objects and pressing the camera button to capture the image. The teacher only prompts the children when needed. She respectfully allows the children to do what they can do independently and only prompts slightly, so that the children are given control over the creation of the slowmation. A high level of teacher intersubjectivity is evident as she supports both children as they contribute differently to the making of the slowmation.

Children's perspectives

The children coordinate their actions both conceptually and socially. The children demonstrate a high level of intersubjectivity between the fairytale narrative, each other and the digital device, as is evident as Timmy controls his urge to press the button of the camera, waiting for Alison as she says 'wait' and always in the context of the fairytale progressing. The fairytale narrative helps Timmy to self-regulate, and Alison to re-produce the narrative in digital form.

What is evident in this case study is that intersubjectivity mattered for both the children and teacher, even though this subjectivity was directed differently. Key here is how the children individually and collectively connected and conceptualised the

(Continued)

(Continued)

creation of a slowmation – it had to be thought about holistically. The technology afforded a level of social interaction between children and a level of collective inter- action, as we might also see when children play together forming a common play narrative. This level of collective interaction and intersubjectivity was necessary if they were to successfully make the slowmation of *The Three Billy Goats Gruff.*

In the next case study, we see how the story narrative with the technology can build across people, time and space.

CASE STUDY 3   *JACK AND THE BEANSTALK*

A group of children aged 3.3–5.3 years and their teachers over a period of three weeks explore the fairytale of *Jack and the Beanstalk*. The teacher has created a Jack's Corner, where a range of props is made available for the children to role-play during the free play period. The teacher and children also plants beans in cups and the teacher supports the children to water and care for the plants and to observe the bean growth. In this context she brings together small groups of children and also works with individuals to represent the growth of the bean as an animation. An example of LL and his teacher during free play time follows.

LL starts to make a slowmation with playdough on a breadboard with the support of his teacher. The slowmation is based on *Jack and the Beanstalk*. LL uses the different coloured playdough that he made earlier to build a slowmation of the beanstalk growing. The teacher draws LL's attention to the science in the slowma- tion by referencing what the beanstalk needs to grow (i.e. sun, water, etc.). As he responds to the teacher's prompts he makes the relevant playdough figure and adds it to the slowmation board. They discuss the growth of the beanstalk by taking a photograph with the iPad by holding it above the board. Another segment is added to the stem, as well as a leaf, and then LL takes another photo of the 'growing beanstalk'. LL asks about the various features of the app (MyCreate) as he is making the slowmation. The teacher responds by explaining each dimension of the app.

Teacher perspectives

The teacher uses the iPad as a tool to help the children to bring together their under- standings by creating a slowmation of bean growth. She draws upon their experi- ences of growing beans, the story reading sessions of the fairytale, and the children's free play with the props in Jack's Corner, to create the conditions for the focus of the slowmation. The digital technology is used to crystallise learning about bean growth.

Children's perspectives

The children have an opportunity to express their understanding about bean growth through making a slowmation. The digital tool allows for a level of abstraction to be mediated through the playdough and through the photographing of the sequence of plant growth, as represented over time through the building of the plant with the playdough.

What is evident here is that the teacher's planning and implementation of the teaching programme was conceptually coherent and enriched the children's thinking through the creation of a slowmation.

The making of a slowmation as a process of abstraction was based on a broad range of experiences in the centre that the teacher had carefully planned and implemented. Learning experiences occurred over days and weeks rather than as a one-off experience. Learning experiences were also spatially featured across the centre in many different ways (e.g. Jack's Corner, growing beans), thus supporting children conceptually with the task of making a slowmation of Jack's or their own, growing bean.

SUMMARY

The three case studies discussed in this chapter highlight how each of the teachers used the digital devices to support their programme, but also that each teacher adopted a different pedagogical approach when planning for, and using digital devices. What is interesting is that the findings revealed a unique series of pedagogical practices across the six teachers for introducing and using digital devices, which are named here as *digital pedagogy*.

KEY DEFINITION

Digital pedagogy

Digital pedagogy captures the special characteristics of how teachers use digital technologies for play, learning and development.

Through following the children's perspective in the context of the teacher's pedagogy, it was possible to draw out the special features of *digital pedagogy*. The characteristics of *digital pedagogy* that have emerged from this study are shown in Table 9.2.

Digital pedagogy captures both the children's perspective and the teacher's perspective as a relational whole. It is not possible to consider the actions of the children independently of the pedagogy of the teacher in an early years setting. Similarly, it is not possible to conceptualise the teacher's pedagogy without thinking about the children's perspective in relation to what the teacher does. As such, *digital pedagogy* must be theorised holistically in early years settings.

The characteristics theorised in Table 9.2 of technological intersubjectivity, distributed technologies, technologically framed narratives, prior experiences infused in the technologies, and virtual placeholders and digital pivots are mostly unique to digital contexts. Together they make up a *digital pedagogy* for early years contexts.

Although a sample of six teachers could never constitute a representative sample, the findings do suggest that a particular pedagogy is evident in these digital contexts. It is argued that more empirical research is needed into the pedagogical practices of teachers using digital devices in the early years, and further, the theorisation of this emergent *digital pedagogy* is urgently needed.

Table 9.2 Characteristics of digital pedagogy.

Digital pedagogy	From the child's perspective	From the teacher's perspective
Technological intersubjectivity: A shared understanding between teachers, children and technologies.	Children engage with other children and the technologies in ways that allow for shared understandings to emerge so as to effectively work towards a commonly understood action.	The teacher is sensitive to what the children do with the technologies, only prompting as needed in order to help build a shared understanding.
Distributed technologies: Technologies are distributed across time and space.	Children meaningfully engage with the technology because the content and concepts are framed across a broad range of activities and over time.	Teachers build a complex and distributed conceptual framing of interlinking activities where the technology is embedded.
Technologically framed narratives: Technologies hold together ideas and content in the form of a conceptual whole.	Children make sense of new content because the technology creates/presents a narrative.	The teacher uses the technology to hold together concepts and content in the form of a narrative. Rather than presenting something, as we might see when reading a book, the teacher supports the collective creation of a narrative.
Prior experiences are infused in the technologies: Technological activity is imbued with possibilities for connecting with and using prior experiences.	Children are given the opportunity to be able to draw upon their prior experiences and growing competence with digital technologies.	*Trusting the technology:* The teacher opens up possibilities for children to use technologies through handing the devices to them, moderating teacher control, and choosing software designed to allow children to direct and change how the devices and apps are used.
Virtual placeholders and digital pivots: Actions and content are captured in digital form that can be used as a pivot for abstracting (Fleer, 2014).	*Virtual placeholders:* Children can capture in digital form aspects of their everyday world, and manipulate this content so as to give new meaning to the digital situation. *Digital pivots:* Children can act 'as if' they are in new situations or simulations. They can also change everyday life by augmenting reality with technologies, creating new play and learning situations.	Teachers support children to capture everyday life through selecting appropriate apps, where imaginary situations are created, but also where apps can augment reality and give new play conditions to children.

Acknowledgements

Special thanks to Sue March (field leader), Megan Adams, Feiyan Chen, Rowan Fleer-Stout, Judith Gomes, Yijun Hao, Madeleine Holland, Hasnat Jahan, Shuhuan Pang, Shukla Sikder, Devi Sukmawati and Pui Ling Wong.

References and further reading

Björk-Willén, P. and Aronsson, K. (2014) Preschoolers' 'animation' of computer games. *Mind, Culture, and Activity* 21(4): 318–336.

Burke, A. and Marsh, J. (eds) (2013) *Children's Virtual Play Worlds*: *Culture, Learning, and Participation.* New York: Peter Lang.

DEEWR (Department of Education, Employment and Workplace Relations) (2009) *Belonging, Being and Becoming: The Early Years Learning Framework for Australia.* Canberra: Commonwealth of Australia.

Fleer, M. (2014) *Theorising Play in the Early Years.* New York: Cambridge University Press.

Fleer, M. (2017) Digital role-play: Creating new conditions for children's play. *Mind, Culture, and Activity* 24(1): 3–17.

Gibbons, A. (2015) Debating digital childhoods: Questions concerning technologies, economies and determinisms. *Open Review of Educational Research* 2(1): 118–127.

Hedegaard, M. (2012) Analyzing children's learning and development in everyday settings from a cultural-historical wholeness approach. *Mind, Culture, and Activity* 19(2): 127–138.

Hinostroza, J.E., Labbé, C. and Matamala, C. (2013) The use of computers in preschools in Chile: Lessons for practitioners and policy designers. *Computers and Education* 68: 96–104.

Hoban, G. and Nielsen, W. (2014) Creating a narrated stop-motion animation to explain science: The affordances of 'Slowmation' for generating discussion. *Teaching and Teacher Education* 42: 68–78.

Kjallander, S. and Moiian, F. (2014). Digital tablets and applications in preschool – Preschoolers' creative transformation of digital design. *Designs for Learning,* 7(1): 10–33.

Marsh, J. (2014) Purposes for literacy in children's use of the online virtual world Club Penguin. *Journal of Research in Reading* 37(2): 179–195.

McKenney, S. and Voogt, J. (2010) Technology and young children: How 4–7 year olds perceive their own use of computers. *Computers in Human Behavior* 26(4): 656–664.

Moore, H.L.C (2014) *Young Children's Play Using Digital Touch-Screen Tablets.* Unpublished PhD thesis, The University of Texas at Austin.

O'Mara, J. and Laidlaw, L. (2011) Living in the iworld: Two literacy researchers reflect on the changing texts and literacy practices of childhood. *English Teaching: Practice and Critique* 10(4): 149–159.

Nolan, J. and McBride, M. (2014) Beyond gamification: Reconceptualizing game-based learning in early childhood environments. *Information, Communication and Society* 17(5): 594–608.

Saçkes, M., Trundle, K.C. and Bell, R.L. (2011) Young children's computer skills development from kindergarten to third grade. *Computers and Education* 57(2): 1698–1704.

Talamo, A., Pozzi, S. and Barbara Mellini, B. (2009) Uniqueness of experience and virtual playworlds: Playing is not just for fun. *Mind, Culture, and Activity* 17(1): 23–41.

Verenikina, I. and Kervin, L. (2011) iPads, digital play, and pre-schoolers. *He Kupu: The Word* 2(5): 4–19. Retrieved from: www.hekupu.ac.nz/index.php?type=journal&issue=15&journal=262 (accessed 27 January 2017).

Vygotsky, L.S. (1966) Play and its role in the mental development of the child. *Voprosy Psikhologii* 12(6): 62–76.

Vygotsky, L.S. (1987) *The Collected Works of L.S. Vygotsky. Problems of General Psychology*, Vol. 1, trans. N. Minick, ed. R.W. Rieber and A.S. Carton. New York: Plenum Press.

Vygotsky, L.S. (1994) The problem of the environment. In R. van der Veer and J. Valsiner (eds), *The Vygotsky Reader*. Oxford: Blackwell pp. 338–354.

Vygotsky, L.S. (1997) *The Collected Works of L.S. Vygotsky. The History of the Development of Higher Mental Functions*, Vol. 4, trans. M.J. Hall, ed. R.W. Rieber. New York: Plenum Press.

Wohlwend, K.E. (2015) One screen, many fingers: Young children's collaborative literacy play with digital puppetry apps and touchscreen technologies. *Theory into Practice* 54(2): 154–162.

Wohlwend, K.E. and Buchholz, B.A. (2014) Paper pterodactyls and popsicle sticks: Expanding school literacy through filmmaking and toymaking. In C. Burnett, J. Davies, G. Merchant and J. Rowsell (eds), *New Literacies around the Globe: Policy and Pedagogy*. Abingdon: Routledge.

Wohlwend, K.E. and Kargin, T. (2013) 'Cause I know how to get friends-plus they like my dancing': (L)earning the nexus of practice in Club Penguin. In A. Burke and J. Marsh (eds), *Children's Virtual Play Worlds: Culture, Learning, and Participation*. New York: Peter Lang, pp. 79–98.

10

TECHNOLOGIES, CHILD-CENTRED PRACTICE AND LISTENING TO CHILDREN

Susan Danby

CHAPTER OVERVIEW

This chapter discusses the generation of observational and interview data with children, how to seek access and participation from children and adults, and how to involve children as knowledgeable research participants within the context of digital childhoods. Underpinning these research practices, and the focus of this chapter, are core research principles to consider when involving young children in research contexts that involve technologies:

- Conceptual understandings of children as competent research participants in an era where digital resources are becoming data collection tools.
- Principles and practices that underpin ethical research with children, considering the role of online data collection and the use of publicly available social media data as well as publishing digital materials.
- Strategies and considerations for researching with children, including how to engage in observational research and in research conversations both with and about technologies.

The previous chapters in this book have pointed to the need for rigorous research evidence about children's interactions with technologies. The authors have talked about the need to consider children's play experiences with technologies and move beyond the focus on causal links between technology use and cognitive development. This chapter offers an insight into how this conceptual shift may be achieved and addresses some key considerations for listening to children about their everyday lives as they engage with digital technologies.

Ethical considerations are at the forefront of any project with children as research participants: the consent process, relationships of power and the challenges in entering and, potentially, affecting the cultures of those children. With examples from ethnographic studies investigating the place of technology in the lives of young children in home and school settings, I examine the directions and affordances of child-centred research, and consider the ethical issues of research with young children.

Many, but not all, studies discussed in this chapter explore children's worlds and their engagement with digital technologies and media. The focus is on how to investigate these worlds, and include practical matters of observational research. Research questions that focus on digital technologies in everyday life might focus on social relationships, and might include, for example:

- How are digital technologies used in everyday activities across home and school contexts?
- How do children participate and engage with others when using digital technologies?
- What relationships do children construct in their everyday interactions with each other and with digital technologies?

These questions allude to the idea that the social and physical environments of home and school are rich and complex settings for understanding children's social interactions with others and with technologies. Thus, in an era where there is increasing access to digital resources and where many children are 'connected' through digital technologies, children's cultures are becoming increasingly complex. The research methods involved in understanding the child's world are similarly complex. This chapter highlights some of those elements that are unique to research with and about technologies.

Conceptual understandings of children as competent research participants in a digital era

Children have a right to be treated as any research participant might, to be seen and heard as competent informants and as interpreters of their everyday worlds (Danby, 2002; Speier, 1973). This perspective recognises that children actively draw on their social interactional resources, and challenges traditional views of childhood as a place where children passively accept or take up adult social structures, including those related to research contexts. Taking a perspective that recognises children as active participants in the research agenda has implications for researching with children.

Working from a stance that children are active research participants leads to explorations of how to engage with children in their roles as research participants (Danby and Farrell, 2004; Danby et al., 2011; Marsh and Richards, 2013). Sometimes known as the 'competence paradigm', this approach recognizes the in situ competence of children. By this, we mean that children are competent in language use and communication strategies in their everyday worlds (Danby, 2002; Hutchby and Moran-Ellis, 1998; Mackay, 1991; Waksler, 1991). This research stance recognises that children have a right to have their voices heard, and to participate and have a say in matters that concern them (Alderson, 2008; LeBlanc, 1995). Recognising children as competent interpreters of their everyday worlds also drives a research agenda that invests in understanding children's lives in the here-and-now (Danby, 2002, 2009; James et al., 1998). The here-and-now for many young children in the West is a digital childhood, and this perspective recognises children's competence with using technologies, in their everyday life and as communication tools.

By shifting the research focus from being a 'child' participant to being a 'research' participant, we can attend to an agenda that takes seriously the involvement of children in research (Danby and Farrell, 2005; Mason and Danby, 2011). In recognising children's everyday competences, Lundy (2007: 933) proposes that four elements be considered in a rights-based model when seeking children's participation:

- Afford children space to be able to express their perspectives.
- Support children to have their perspectives heard.
- Present children's perspectives to audiences (for example, through talk, drawings, actions).
- Follow up and act on, when possible, children's perspectives.

These four elements, together, highlight that research that involves children as participants (through observation, interview, drawings, and so on) is a thoughtful undertaking that has implications in both the conduct, and dissemination, of the research findings. When we add technological tools into the mix, we see huge possibilities to shape the above model of participation in light of digital childhoods.

An increasing number of studies recognise children as active research participants. Below are brief descriptions of four studies that, each in their own way, recognise children's agency in the research process:

1. In a UK study of children's school playground rhymes and games, Marsh and Richards (2013) discuss how they used a children's panel that consisted of some children from the school and members of the research team. They met regularly to consider data collection methods and analysis. The children participated by recording playground rhymes and games, writing field notes to capture playground observations, and interviewing other children about their playground activities.
2. In a study of children's social interactions, Arnott (2013) showed in her UK study how the preschool-aged children used their voices to provide insights into how they constructed social status roles using technologies. Their agency was shown in the identities they constructed among their peers.
3. An Australian study of children explored how children participated in literacy practices when using technology (Kervin and Mantei, 2009). In creating literacy texts, the children showed and described their insights on this literacy learning experience. They talked about how to navigate the tool bar, bookmark sites, find information and revisit their plans, and how they worked collaboratively. They designed their own home pages and designed plans.

4. An Australian study of a novice researcher who undertook interviews with young children examined how she prepared for the interview and managed the interview context (Danby et al., 2011). Recognising the theoretical principle that young children are competent informants, it was possible to show how young children actively participate in the research process as research participants. This article provides examples from an interview with a young child to show how the use of an artefact can help both the researcher and child feel comfortable and to encourage more extended conversations.

Although each study had a different purpose and each was framed within different conceptual and methodological frameworks, together they highlight that child participation in research can be understood as located on a continuum, from studies that seek and value children's perspectives, through to studies that involve children as co-researchers. This evidence is applicable to understanding children's everyday uses of technologies, and also to understanding the place of involving children as co-researchers while using technologies for data collection purposes.

Ethical research with children

Ethical principles and practices underpin research activities. Previously, children's views typically were not sought, and adults such as parents and teachers were asked to speak on behalf of children. With research perspectives changing, however, children are now increasingly being involved as research participants. Their involvement requires consent for their involvement and usually there a number of gatekeepers who control this process.

Once a research project is conceptualised, there are a number of ethical procedures that require attention before any data collection can take place. Well-known gatekeepers include institutional approval, which is usually granted through ethical committees. If attached to a university, the university ethical committee has to provide approval, as do participating organisations that may include schools, playgroups, hospitals and other clinical settings. Each institution has its own set of guidelines and regulations that meet national and local legislative and ethical requirements. The first step is to become knowledgeable about these requirements. Increasingly, there are ethics advisors within institutions to help guide this process. There may be more than one institution involved, such as a university and a school. Once the relevant institutions have provided formal consent, the next step is to invite research participants.

Yet in the digital and information era, the concept of gatekeepers and access to data are changing as more and more children and young people are engaging with internet-enabled activities (Australian Bureau of Statistics, 2014; Chaudron, 2015; Rideout, 2013), leaving a digital footprint. These data become publicly available and often the subject of research data collection, potentially without the children and young people realising. This situation poses new considerations for researchers in order to maintain an ethically sound approach to involving young children in the research process. While it may be argued that such practices are not relevant to young children because many online materials and social media sites are age restricted, it is clear that children are engaging with these spaces at young ages and, often parents are creating a digital presence on behalf of their children, long before children are aware of it.

There are a number of things to consider when undertaking research with children, as the following subsection shows.

Gatekeepers

Gatekeepers have important roles in managing the process of ethical research, and are involved in every aspect of the research. This is particularly important in light of research in the internet and digital age. From the conceptualisation phase of the study, the researcher has to be aware of the legislation relevant to conducting the research as understanding consent and participant access protocols are necessary preconditions before any research can take place. Gatekeepers include institutional partners (e.g. university ethics committees and education departments). Once these partners provide consent for the study, the consent process next involves participants who may be involved in the research. When the research involves children, the consent process typically involves the consent of the child's parents or caregivers as well as the children's own assent. The main points to consider are:

- Know the relevant legislation related to research ethics.
- Seek ethical approval for the study from University and the Institutional ethical committees.
- Develop consent and information packages that address key ethical matters.
- Seek formal consent from participants.
- Recognise that participants are gatekeepers of their own ongoing consent and assent, and the researcher's role is to be sensitive to these matters.

In seeking to involve children in the research process ethically, whether it relates to their use of digital technologies or some other aspects of their lives and experiences, the opening conversations held with young children are important in establishing the relationship between the researcher and the child. In the interview fragment shown below, parents had already given written permission for their child to be involved, and the child had also given her written assent, which was marked with a symbol or pseudonym on a consent form designed specifically for them (see Danby and Farrell, 2005). The interview fragment shows how the researcher checks that the child is still comfortable with being involved in the study, and is clear about what her participation in the research project means.

In Fragment 1, reproduced from Danby and Farrell (2005: 59–60), Lilly, provides her account for how she feels about being actively involved in the research process.

Fragment 1 (Danby and Farrell, 2005: 59–60)

Researcher: So you thought that it was a good thing to have to do?
Lilly: Yeah.
Researcher: And what did your parents think about you signing?

Lilly:	Cause then they know that I wanna do it not just them.
Researcher:	That's right.
Lilly:	Because if you just have your parents signing it sorta seems like some children don't even wanna do it they just want (.) their parents just want (.) to do to do it so, this way you have to get y- y children to actually do it to make sure that you want to do it.
Researcher:	Mhmmm mhmmm. Andd why did you want to do the study?
Lilly:	Uhmmmm I don't know, I just like to try things.

As Danby and Farrell (2005) point out, the researcher oriented to Lilly as a research participant, so that she had the final say in whether or not she participated in the research project. Her response recognises that she has agency in terms of her active involvement. Children's active participation as researchers begins with their knowing about the research, how they might contribute to that research, and their active agreement to be involved.

The concepts of active agreement and involvement, however, are evolving and becoming even more complex in light of digital childhoods. For example, clarification of the child's understanding is vital considering contemporary approaches to research where new methods of data dissemination may mean that children are immortalised in pictorial, audio or video media. An ethical approach is one where children are made aware of the potential ramifications of their digital images being preserved in this way, and to consider what might be the consequences for their future leisure and working lives if they are identifiable in research data, particularly in light of the current movement towards open access data.

Participation is always an ongoing enterprise. Children may indicate periodically that they wish not to be video recorded at particular times. For example, in one classroom where I observed young children's engagement using digital technologies, I video recorded children reading aloud the digital story that they had produced. One child stumbled over a few words while she read her story. Later in the day, she came to me and asked me not to use that particular video recording in my study, and I reassured her that I would not show that video to anyone. Being sensitive to children's wishes includes listening when they say that they do not want to participate, and also requires a sensitivity to understanding children's actions. For example, if children find private spaces where the researcher is not able to observe, the message being given by the participants is that the children wish to keep their activity within a private space. Researcher sensitivity to both spoken and unspoken requests requires careful 'listening' by the researcher and a recognition of child-centred practices that support the child to have a say about matters that affect them.

In the same study of children's engagement using digital technologies, I observed family interactions and the flow of digital technologies in families' everyday lives. On a home visit with one family, Anna (a pseudonym that she had selected herself) had talked to me about how she liked using email to communicate with her mother. As she was one of four siblings, she valued these one-on-one interactions. I asked Anna would she feel comfortable with sharing some examples of her email communication, and she agreed. This process also involved Anna's mother as we negotiated how we might undertake forwarding emails on to me. Anna managed the process by letting her mother know which emails her mother could forward on to me. I provide an example of an email chain in Figure 10.1, to show how digital communication can build family relationships. The figure shows how Anna stays in touch with her mother, telling her about a recent school result.

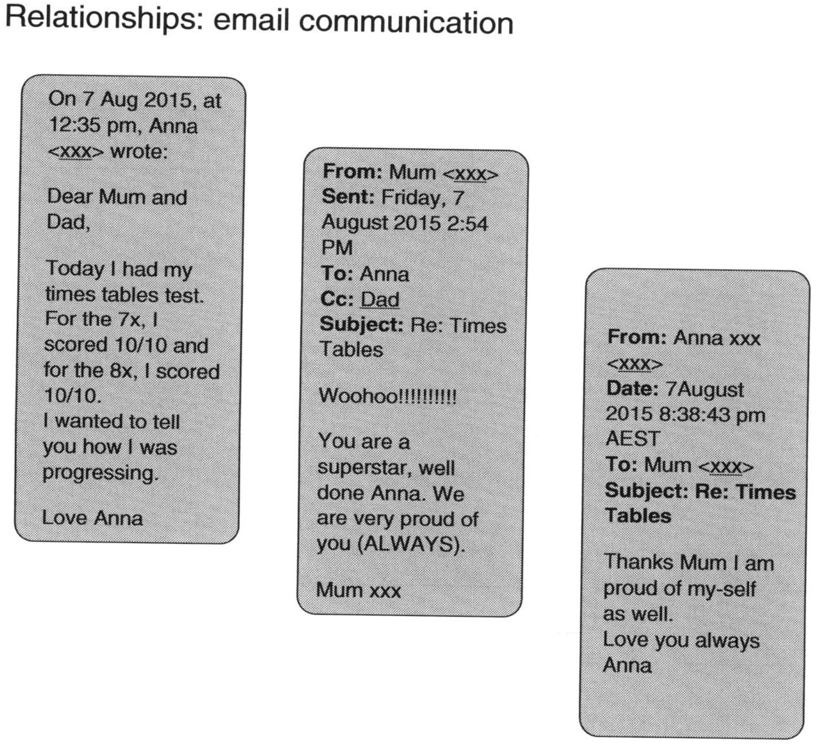

Relationships: email communication

On 7 Aug 2015, at 12:35 pm, Anna <xxx> wrote:

Dear Mum and Dad,

Today I had my times tables test. For the 7x, I scored 10/10 and for the 8x, I scored 10/10.
I wanted to tell you how I was progressing.

Love Anna

From: Mum <xxx>
Sent: Friday, 7 August 2015 2:54 PM
To: Anna
Cc: Dad
Subject: Re: Times Tables

Woohoo!!!!!!!!!

You are a superstar, well done Anna. We are very proud of you (ALWAYS).

Mum xxx

From: Anna xxx <xxx>
Date: 7August 2015 8:38:43 pm AEST
To: Mum <xxx>
Subject: Re: Times Tables

Thanks Mum I am proud of my-self as well.
Love you always Anna

Figure 10.1   Email chain showing family communication.

The essence of undertaking research with participants, including with children, is to ensure that all participants, research team members and research participants alike, build trusting and transparent relationships. In relation to the email example, I had been visiting the family for over two years, making several visits a year, and spending time participating in family life. As part of that trust relationship, we were able to consider the implications of sharing data publicly, within academic circles and across internet sites more broadly, addressing those issues of gatekeepership and immortalisation of data online highlighted above.

Engaging in observational research and research converstaions

This section discusses two approaches to generating data in research studies. The first method involves collecting observational data, often using video or audio technologies where the researcher attempts to capture as much as possible of people's everyday interactions. A close observation of children's talk and interaction shows their understandings and everyday practices. The second method involves undertaking interviews to gain understanding of participants' perspectives through their accounts. There are also many other methods to collect data with technologies that can afford children a direct role in the data collection process and as co-researcher, such as screen snapshots of the computer screen, photographs, drawings, completion of tasks and writing samples, but these are not the focus in this chapter.

Observational research provides understandings of what participants are saying and doing. In studies of children using digital technologies, my interest is in the flow of everyday family and school life and the use of digital devices. This interest becomes translated into research that explores how children co-construct their everyday interactions in home and school settings. Video recording everyday interactions is one way to re-watch many times the interactions taking place. This opportunity to replay the video recorded interactions means that it is possible to look for the finer details of interactions that are so often missed in simply observing everyday actions. To understand what is happening among the participants, by watching replays and being able to slow down the video recording, means that features of talk and action, such as silences in the talk, gestures such as pointing to the screen and other actions such as laughing and frowning can be observed, and these help to understand what is happening moment-by-moment (Danby et al., 2013; Heath et al., 2010; Mehan, 1993).

Observational data of family life require great sensitivity and strategies to ensure that families feel comfortable with the process. A study by Danby et al. (2013) explored young children's engagement with mobile technologies in home contexts. In this study, the father and his two children, one aged 18 months and one aged 3 years, were using apps on mobile devices, as they lay in bed on a Sunday morning. The interaction shows how the father calibrated his questions to the children's levels of interest and language development. The family were invited to video record their everyday interactions using digital devices and, in this way, they were able to select which family experiences they wished to record and share with the researchers. It is the researchers' responsibility to respectfully and ethically consider, with family members, matters such as permission for the inclusion of family images and selective use of video recorded fragments in contexts such as research and teaching.

In educational contexts, ethical and practical considerations also require careful negotiation with stakeholders and research participants. A recent Australian study investigated how two boys, aged 4 years, used the application Google Earth (Danby et al., 2016). Parents and children, as well as the teacher and school organisation, each provided consent to video record their child's classroom activities. The parents of one child gave permission for the child to be included in the study, but did not give permission for his image to be used. This meant that brief fragments that included this child were video edited so that his image was blurred, and he was not recognisable. Written transcripts of his actions, however, were available as data, as consented to by his parents and the child. This study video recorded what the children were doing when they were using particular programs or applications. Copyright considerations prevented the inclusion of images of Google Earth in printed form. Digital online images, however, may be used if there is written authorisation to use images for publication. For example, Ekberg and colleagues were able to use screen images for which they had sought and received copyright permission (Ekberg et al., 2016).

Research conversations with children involve listening to children, respecting their right as research participants, building on relationships of trust and rapport, and drawing on strategies to show that the researcher is listening to them. In preparation for the research interview, the researcher should address the following actions:

- Plan for the interview and build familiar contexts where the children and the interviewer feel comfortable.
- Consider how an artefact may act as a resource for encouraging extended conversations.
- Recognise children's participation in the research process (Danby et al., 2011).

Fragment 2 begins at the start of an interview between a novice interviewer and a preschool-aged child called Tammy (Danby et al., 2011). This fragment shows how the novice interviewer rushes to start asking questions of the child participant, and shows how the participant responds.

Fragment 2 (Excerpt 2, in Danby et al., 2011: 76)

```
1. R:      Okay °so Tammy° What does being a friend mean to you
2. → T:    Um being ↑nice
3. R:      Being ↑nice °anything else°
4. → T:    Not saying naughty ↑<words>=
5. R:      =Mmm
6.                 (2.0)
7. → R:    so a friend is somebody that's nice to ↑you
8.                 (2.0)
9. T:      ((Nods her head))
```

As pointed out by Danby et al. (2011), the interviewer rushes first to ask her probing questions without first beginning with any social talk that might encourage Tammy to feel comfortable with the interview as it unfolds. In line 1, the interviewer does attempt to show that it is Tammy's views that are being sought, shown by her reference using the pronoun 'you'. Tammy's response, with an upward inflection, suggests that Tammy is searching for an answer the interviewer might be seeking. As the conversation proceeds turn by turn, the interviewer seems to pick up on Tammy's talk when it is about niceness (lines 2, 3, 8) but does not follow up when Tammy mentions that being a friend is 'not saying naughty words' (line 4). The researcher does not probe this point further.

Engaging children in conversations for research purposes requires the researcher to be finely tuned into what is being discussed to encourage more elaborated conversations (Danby et al., 2011).

One way to build the study's reliability is for the researcher to provide empirical evidence. Such documentation might consist of detailed field notes, audio or video fragments and detailed transcripts that capture the episode (Peräkylä, 1997; Silverman, 2013). Detailed transcribed extracts of video recordings of children's everyday experiences can make visible to others the participants' talk and actions in ways that the reader can understand how the interaction unfolded moment-by-moment. Here we see how technologies become both a data collection tool but also the subject of the investigation.

In this chapter, so far, discussion has included some strategies and practices for researchers to consider when involving young children. These processes, however, are not a series of steps or recipes for how to conduct ethical research with and about technologies. Every action we do as researchers requires us to actively consider that action and to consider how those actions, and the actions of the participants, are open to reflection in terms of how such actions might affect others (Davies, 2014). This process of researcher reflection and reflexivity is an essential research tool for those making sense of children's everyday experiences, and are core elements when undertaking ethical research with young children. Our work as researchers requires us to bring some lens or light to shine on how we generate and analyse data, and manage the research enterprise, from the earliest conceptualisations of the study, through to ethical considerations throughout the entire project and interactions with gatekeepers and participants, and in some cases with the digital media.

One aspect of research rarely discussed is what happens when the study is completed. Underpinning the research process is a commitment to considering the benefit for the participants of the study, and this means considering practical and applied ways to recognise their involvement. In one research project that invited families to video record their everyday practices of using technologies at home, those families received an external hard drive with a compilation of that family's video recorded episodes. On a broader scale, new understandings drawn from the findings of the research may be shared with others in many ways, including through presentations, publications and workshops. For practitioner/action researchers, new understandings become incorporated into the everyday practices of classroom life. These considerations of the dissemination of digital data respect the rights of the children involved (Third et al., 2014).

--------------------| **SUMMARY** |--

This chapter has outlined key considerations to consider when investigating how young children engage with digital technologies, and how we can best listen to children to understand their perspectives with technologies. Underpinning the strategies and practices discussed here regarding ethical research are three overarching principles:

- Negotiated and ongoing relationships between researchers and children supported by child-centred practices, including internet-enabled relationships and communications.
- Recognition that many children and young people are informants of their everyday digital lives and are skilful technology users.
- Reflexive approaches consider how researchers are engaging in the research enterprise in light of the changes associated with the digital era.

Undertaking research is complex and time-consuming, and requires knowledge of a research process that recognises ethical approaches, data generation and analysis methods, and, most importantly, conceptual underpinnings to inform and frame the study.

Acknowledgements

ARC FT1210731, DP0452493, DP0666254 and DP1114227 were funded by the Australian Research Council. All studies have ethical approval by Queensland University of Technology's University Human Research Ethics Committee. Thank you to the children and young people, parents and teachers for their participation in these studies. Thank you also to the research teams involved in these studies.

References and further reading

Alderson, P. (2008) *Young Children's Rights: Exploring Beliefs, Principles and Practice*. London: Jessica Kingsley.

Arnott, L. (2013) Are we allowed to blink? Young children's leadership and ownership while mediating interactions around technologies. *International Journal of Early Years Education* 21(1): 97–115.

Australian Bureau of Statistics (2014). 8146.0 – Household use of information technology, Australia, 2012–13. Retrieved from: www.abs.gov.au/ausstats/abs@.nsf/Lookup/8146.0Chapter12012-13 (accessed 27 January 2017).

Chaudron, S. (2015) *Young Children (0–8) and Digital Technology: A Qualitative Exploratory Study Across Seven Countries*. Retrieved from: publications.jrc.ec.europa.eu/repository/bitstream/JRC93239/lbna27052enn.pdf (accessed 27 January 2017).

Danby, S. (2002) The communicative competence of young children. *Australian Journal of Early Childhood* 27(3): 25–30.

Danby, S. (2009) Childhood and social interaction in everyday life: An epilogue. *Journal of Pragmatics* 41(8): 1596–1599.

Danby, S. and Farrell, A. (2004) Accounting for young children's competence in educational research: New perspectives on research ethics. *Australian Educational Researcher* 31(3): 35–50.

Danby, S. and Farrell, A. (2005) Opening the research conversation. In A. Farrell (ed.), *Ethical Research with Children*. Milton Keynes: Open University Press, pp. 49–67.

Danby, S., Ewing, L. and Thorpe, K. (2011) The novice researcher: Interviewing young children. *Qualitative Inquiry* 17(1): 74–84.

Danby, S., Davidson, C., Theobald, M., et al. (2013) Talk in activity during young children's use of digital technologies at home. *Australian Journal of Communication* 40(2): 83–99.

Danby, S., Davidson, C., Ekberg, S., et al. (2016) 'Let's see if you can see me': Making connections with Google Earth™ in a preschool classroom. *Children's Geographies* 14(2): 14 1–157.

Davies, B. (2014) *Listening to Children: Being and Becoming*. London: Routledge.

Ekberg, S., Danby, S., Davidson, C. and Thorpe, K.J. (2016) Identifying and addressing equivocal trouble in understanding within classroom interaction. *Discourse Studies* 18(1): 3–24.

Heath, C., Hindmarsh, J. and Luff, P. (2010) *Video in Qualitative Research: Analysing Social Interaction in Everyday Life*. Los Angeles, CA: Sage.

Hutchby, I. and Moran-Ellis, J. (1998) Situating children's social competence. In I. Hutchby and J. Moran-Ellis (eds), *Children and Social Competence: Arenas of Action*. London: Falmer Press, pp. 7–26.

James, A., Jenks, C. and Prout, A. (1998) *Theorizing Childhood*. Cambridge: Polity Press.

Kervin, L. and Mantei, J. (2009) Using computers to support children as authors: An examination of three cases. *Technology, Pedagogy and Education* 18(1): 19–32.

LeBlanc, L.J. (1995) *The Convention on the Rights of the Child: United Nations Lawmaking on Human Rights*. Lincoln: University of Nebraska Press.

Lundy, L. (2007) 'Voice' is not enough: Conceptualising Article 12 of the United Nations Convention on the Rights of the Child. *British Educational Research Journal* 33(6): 927–942.

Mackay, R.W. (1991) Conceptions of children and models of socialization. In F.C. Waksler (ed.), *Studying the Social Worlds of Children: Sociological Readings*. London: Falmer Press, pp. 23–37.

Marsh, J. and Richards, C. (2013) Children as researchers. In R. Willett, C. Richards, J. Marsh, et al. (eds), *Children, Media and Playground Cultures: Ethnographic Studies of Playground Playtimes*. New York: Palgrave Macmillan, pp. 51–67.

Mason, J. and Danby, S. (2011) Editorial to special issue: Children as experts in their lives: Child inclusive research. *Child Indicators Research* 4(2): 185–189.

Mehan, H. (1993) Why I like to look: On the use of videotape as an instrument in educational research. In M. Schratz (ed.), *Qualitative Voices in Educational Research*. London: Falmer Press, pp. 93–105.

Peräkylä, A. (1997) Reliability and validity in research based on transcripts. In D. Silverman (ed.), *Qualitative Research: Theory, Method and Practice*. London: Sage, pp. 201–220.

Rideout, V. (2013) *Zero to Eight: Children's Media Use in America 2013*. Retrieved from: www.commonsensemedia.org/research/zero-to-eight-childrens-media-use-in-america-2013 (accessed 27 January 2017).

Silverman, D. (2013) *Doing Qualitative Research*, 4th edn. London: Sage.

Speier, M. (1973) *How to Observe Face-to-Face Communication: A Sociological Introduction*. Pacific Palisades, CA: Goodyear Publishing Company.

Third, A., Bellerose, D., Dawkins, U., et al. (2014) *Children's Rights in the Digital Age: A Download from Children around the World*. Melbourne: Young and Well Cooperative Research Centre. Retrieved from: youngandwellcrc.org.au

Waksler, F.C. (1991) Studying children: Phenomenological insights. In F.C. Waksler (ed.), *Studying the Social Worlds of Children: Sociological Readings*. London: Falmer Press, pp. 60–69.

INDEX

Printed in Great Britain
by Amazon